Celebrating with MOTHER GOOSE

Ah Mother Goose,

When her tummy used to grumble,

Would pop into the kitchen

To make a tart or crumble.

And Mother Goose's flock of chicks,

Not to be ignored,

Would not leave her tasty kitchen

Til' every recipe was explored!

- Lacey Mauritz

FOREWORD

What do I love about *Celebrating with Mother Goose: Snacks, Sweets & Sips*? In short, everything!

Some of my most treasured memories of growing up were in the kitchen cooking with my parents. Families can use this beautiful book to explore the world of Mother Goose in the traditional read-the-rhyme-aloud and look-at-the-illustrations kind of ~~way and in a new way,~~ cooking foods inspired by the rhymes. You'll pull out this book for everyday snacks and pass it around during weekends and holidays for special drinks and desserts. These rhymes and recipes will be interwoven with your family traditions and become some of your children's favorite memories.

Other children's cookbooks tend to focus on kids cooking for themselves or on parents preparing separate "kid food" without their children's input or involvement. *Celebrating with Mother Goose* is not that kind of cookbook. This book (like its companion, *Cooking with Mother Goose*) encourages parents to cook with their children, thus including them in the process of making delicious food. Studies show that kids eat a more varied and balanced diet when they participate in meal preparation. Lacey calls out meaningful tasks a child can do in each recipe in the "Kids Can" sections, so parents can know exactly how their kids can safely help. And, likewise, she highlights areas where parents need to supervise in the "Watch Out For" sections.

Children as young as 2 years old will learn to explore ingredients like avocados, eggs, raspberries and spices. This book is filled with recipes that are kid-friendly but also interesting, so mom, dad and friends also want to participate in the creation. The food is delicious, appealing and each recipe starts with whole food ingredients. There are three challenge levels so that both a beginner and a chef-super-mom or dad and their kids can make these foods with confidence and share the experience. There are many more easy recipes, labeled "Piece of Cake", than any other recipe category.

Lacey includes advice along with strategies to make cooking fun so parents feel good about (and understand a bit of the science behind) the food choices they make for themselves and their children. You'll also find tips relevant to families with young children like how to reduce picky eating, how to handle food likes and dislikes and the benefits of recipe ingredients to health—all in a beautiful presentation with whimsical nursery rhyme characters the whole family will love.

In the end, this book is a treasure that will be used by moms, dads, siblings, aunts, uncles, cousins and grandparents and then passed down to the next generations to come.
I know you will enjoy using the recipes often to create special Snacks, Sweets & Sips as well as your own lasting memories with your family in the kitchen!

Catherine Christie, PhD, RDN, LDN

Celebrating with MOTHER GOOSE

BY

LACEY J. MAURITZ, RDN

SNACKS, SWEETS  SIPS

Nursery rhymes and the recipes they inspire
from a dedicated mom-dietitian.

TABLE OF CONTENTS

ACKNOWLEDGEMENTS

Thanks to my incredible family and amazing friends! Your encouragement and belief that families need this book gave me the pluck and creativity to make *Celebrating with Mother Goose* real.

Of course, I want to thank my boys, Axel and Rex (and you too, Todd). You are the reason behind everything that I do. I love you.

Eleanor and Edward, the world would see an entirely different book had it not been for our friendship! The talent and support of your mum (or Granny as Ed calls her) and the entire family have been incredible. I don't think another grandmother on the planet could create the whimsical, wild and weird drawings for these rhymes. Jacqueline, as they say in Chile, *¡te pasaste!* (You've outdone yourself!)

To my parents, who gave me both the foundation to dream and the support to achieve them, y'all are wonderful. To my in-laws for their unwavering support, you rock!

To my sister and my new niece, baby Hazel, I can't wait to read you rhymes from this book and get into the kitchen together.

To all the contributors, thank you so much for sharing strategies, ideas and recipes so we could make the food in this book the best it could be.

Wendy Bazilian, DrPH, RDN, and Cathy Christie, PhD, RDN, LDN, as dietitians and mothers, we live the reality on these pages! Your mentorship, encouragement and enthusiasm for the health and literacy of young people has given me the courage to share this book with the world.

To my editor, Sarah, and designer, Stockton, I still pinch myself that you agreed to do this project. The coaching, the reading (the re-reading), the designing (and re-designing) and the laughs we had figuring it all out made the process both fun and productive. Sarah, you always advise to "use only the amount of words you need to say what you need to say. No more. No less."

So, in that spirit, to everyone who touched the making of this book and to everyone who picks it up, I say, with exactly the right amount of words,

THANK YOU!

CONTRIBUTORS

AXEL KURZIUS MAURITZ AND REX HARRISON MAURITZ

These littles, my boys, ate every recipe in this book (and taste-tested plenty that didn't make the cut)! I started this project when Axel (on the left) had just turned 4 years old and Rex (on the right) was 2½. Together, they've shown me just what **Kids Can** do and what Todd and I need to **Watch Out For** when we are making meals together.

Celebrating with Mother Goose is full of their special requests (**Crab Cakes** and **Mama's Apple Pie**) and advice on how to handle the real-life challenges of what we eat between meals, when we have dessert and what we serve on special occasions. This dynamic duo has pushed me to put my best food forward. They have inspired me to compile practical, science-based nutritional guidance and share "we-lived-through-this-and-you-will-too" stories. It's thanks to them that this book exists. I couldn't ask for better partners!

To find out more about Axel and Rex, keep in touch with me.
These dudes are too young for social media!

JACQUELINE TAYLOR

Jacqueline (Jaq) is a writer and self-taught artist based out of the UK. She is the loving grandmother of Edward Williams, my son's best friend, and an honorary member of our family. Jaq brought *Celebrating with Mother Goose* to life through her art and creativity; I cannot imagine writing this book without her. Jaq has lent her talents to various private story collections, and this is our second time collaborating together.

When Jaq is away from her paints, she spends time outdoors taking satisfaction from the plants and creatures around her. The natural world is her inspiration, from a ladybird landing on her arm to the shade of an oak tree on a summer day.

Find out more about Jacqueline
www.storybooknutrition.com

SILVANA CARBAJAL

Silvana bakes, cooks and tablescapes! She's a self-taught culinary powerhouse and my go-to gal for beautiful, delicious treats. From baptisms to birthdays, class picnics to Christmas morning, no one in Chile makes better cakes, cookies and pastries for celebrating life's sweetest moments. Silvana's background in Peruvian, Canadian and Chilean cuisines gives her food and her table global appeal and her generous heart is poured into everything she makes. Her collaboration in this book was invaluable. If you want to sample some of the recipes we've put our heads together on, see **Chocolate Cake Truffles** (p. 139), **Profiteroles** (p. 141), **Maple Bacon Cake** (p. 147).

Find out more about Silvana
@silvanabakes · www.silvanabakescooksandtablescapes.com

RACHAEL RYDBECK

Is a Le Cordon Bleu trained culinary instructor with over 15 years experience teaching classes to cooks of all skill levels. Her passion is to demystify cooking so that anyone can whip up a simple and satisfying meal. Rachael is also a mom of two and uses her firsthand experience feeding young people to inspire our work on recipes like **Kook-a-Bear Fruit Gummies** (p. 113), **Fruit Leathers** (p. 109) and **Rosemary Crackers** (p. 75). She's also been a clutch recipe-tester for this book.

Find out more about Rachael
@cookingwithrachael · www.cookingwithrachael.com

ANTONIO MUÑOZ

Not every bartender lends their talents to a children's book, but Antonio stepped out from behind the bar to create signature, kid-friendly drinks inspired by the rhymes and recipes in this cookbook. Developing the mocktail recipes in *Celebrating with Mother Goose* was a super fun (and refreshing) way to collaborate. The best part is each non-alcoholic drink we made pairs nicely with the food in this book and in my first book, *Cooking with Mother Goose.* Find them all starting on page 190.

Salud! (Cheers!)

Find out more about Antonio
@elartedelamezcla

TO YOU, THE PARENT ABOUT TO TAKE YOUR CHILDREN ON A JOURNEY IN THE KITCHEN...

Welcome back! *Celebrating with Mother Goose* is your go-to guide for everyday food, parties and special occasions. It's a collection of our favorite snacks, sweets and sips to share with friends, satisfy you between meals, and make the sweet moments in life even tastier. There's also an entire chapter dedicated to crafts and activities, so your little can explore fresh, healthy food on their own terms.

You'll find more of what you loved from *Cooking with Mother Goose:* beautifully illustrated nursery rhymes and tasty, nutritious recipes with photos. Expect to make precious memories, lots of little messes, and create a positive relationship between your little ones, cooking and food.

Children can safely participate in every recipe. Just read the **Kids Can** section on each recipe page to see how. And littles who aren't ready to cook aren't left out. They can look at the pictures and read (or listen to) the rhymes. Plus, every family needs a Taster to give a "thumbs-up" when we get the recipe just right.

If you're motivated and ready to dive right into cooking, baking and mixing, go ahead and skip forward a couple of pages, directly to the "**How to Use This Book**" section. Reading that first will ensure you and your family get the most out of this book. If you are a new friend and don't know me from *Cooking with Mother Goose*, you may be wondering who I am and why I spent the last two years elbow-deep in nursery rhymes and lots and lots of cooking.

In that case, please allow me to introduce myself and my silly, sometimes chaotic, but oh, so beautiful little family.

MY FAMILY (YOUR TEST KITCHEN) IS THE REASON I LOVE HEALTHY COOKING

A LITTLE BIT ABOUT MY FAMILY

I'm a parent just like you. I want the same things for my kids that you want for yours: happiness, health and the certainty that they are loved more than they could ever comprehend. And of course, I want them to have the healthiest possible relationship with food—including snacks and dessert.

Rex and Axel, my two boys, are at the center of Todd's (my husband) and my world. In our home, food is the beginning of adventure. It's where we learn about other cultures, how to be brave and to try things we're unsure of. In the kitchen, it's OK to get our hands dirty. It's where we fill our tummies with yummy foods and our hearts with happy memories.

I grew up in New Orleans, Louisiana and until recently we lived in Santiago, Chile. Now we live in Florida, but you'll find a lot of Creole and South American influence in my recipes. By education and profession, I'm a Registered Dietitian Nutritionist and have been since 2014 when I found my passion for family and child nutrition. I've always believed that, as a dietitian, I have to know how to prepare and serve food to teach people about nutrition and cooking. At the end of the day, my favorite way to support families is by balancing eating with enjoyment.

Celebrating with Mother Goose is my fourth parent-child cookbook and nutrition handbook. It's the companion to *Cooking with Mother Goose*, a collection of rhymes and recipes designed to support healthy food relationships through delicious family-friendly meals. My first two cookbooks, *Eat! Play! Cook!* and *¡Vamos a Cocinar!*, are directed to little eaters 6 months old and up. Together, these books represent the culmination of my influences, experiences, education and love of spending time in the kitchen and at the table with my family.

REX, AXEL, ZOEY AND SOREN
READING MOTHER GOOSE STORIES

WHY MOTHER GOOSE?

The idea came to me one night during our bedtime routine. I'm guessing that like you, reading to my kids before bed has been important since they were born. One night, as we read through *Little Miss Muffet, Polly Put The Kettle On* and *Kookaburra*, it struck me just how many Mother Goose rhymes involve food.

Maybe the connection came to me because I'm a dietitian, or maybe my mind drifted to the kitchen because I love to cook and eat tasty foods. Whatever the reason, drift it did, and that's when the idea for this book was born.

So, I got to work reading and thinking about those classic nursery rhymes and creating recipes that bring food from Mother Goose's world into ours.

Each one of the recipes is inspired by a rhyme. I let Mother Goose be my guide as I challenged not just my culinary—but my dietitian-mom mind to dream up new dishes. Some inspirations are quite literal: **Apple Pie** for the rhyme of the same name, and **Braided Egg Bun**s to celebrate *Hot Cross Buns*.

With other rhymes, I became a bit more creative—the snow in *A Pillow Shaken*, inspired **Meringue Cookies** while *Curdy, Curdy Custard* suggested **Hazelnut Tapioca**.

The goal of this book is straightforward and the benefits are infinite: to bring parents and their littles together around food and cooking. From reducing risks of childhood obesity to ensuring a happy relationship with food into adulthood—coming together to experience meals from preparation to final plate carves out space for adventure, love, imagination and nourishment in all its forms.

Throughout this book, you'll find a variety of ways to involve your child in making meals. From reading the rhymes together and experiencing food with all five senses, to helping prep ingredients, I hope these recipes will nurture your family long after your children leave Mother Goose behind in favor of more rigorous literature.

I'll see you in the kitchen,

Lacey

NUTRITION: CREATING HEALTHY RELATIONSHIPS WITH FOOD

Teaching children and parents how to eat well is what I do for a living—it's my profession and my passion. And I believe a baseline level of understanding about our relationship to food helps parents create an environment of health and enjoyment for their children.

Kids learn more about food and eating during this time than any other time in their life. For this reason, allow me to briefly explain the behaviors, attitudes, beliefs, norms and routines that we can model to our children in a way that encourages them to take the lead and eat intuitively.

BUILDING A FRAMEWORK OF TRUST

Snacks and sugary foods are a part of the modern world. From birthday parties to sports camps to their best friend's pantry, our children are exposed to a wide assortment of processed foods, candies and sugar-filled beverages. One of the best tools we can give our children is exposure to sweet and snack-type foods within our home so they can learn to eat them in moderation and make them from whole ingredients.

Respecting our children to stop when they are full and to reach for nutritious foods more often than not, means letting them experience the healthy and the not-so-healthy genre of snack-food and dessert. Kids who learn to eat these foods mindfully as part of a balanced diet tend to see these foods as just that—part of a balanced diet.

Cookies, for example, are not bad, and eating a cookie does not make a child "bad." **There are no "good foods" or "bad foods."** We eat some food groups every day—like fruits and vegetables, whole grains, protein and dairy. We eat other foods less frequently—like cakes, ice creams and chips. But no foods are prohibited. Like vegetables and whole grains, sweets and snacks have a place in our lives and at our table. Making snacks and sweets as delicious as possible—and healthy too—is what *Celebrating with Mother Goose* is all about.

CLOSED FIST

A closed fist is about the recommended size for a serving of pasta, rice, cereal, vegetables and fruit.

PALM OF HAND

A meat or protein serving should be about as big as the palm of your open hand.

NUTRITION: CREATING HEALTHY RELATIONSHIPS WITH FOOD

Look at the photo on the left.

See the size difference between the little hand and the grown-up one?
Little hands need less food, bigger hands need more food.

SERVINGS OR PORTIONS

Most recipes in this book are shown plated in their entirety to encourage
parents to serve meals and snacks family-style since it brings the family
together and different members will need different portions.

The amount that you eat is called a **portion**. The yield of the recipe is
measured in **servings**. You can have one serving, two servings or even
four servings as your portion. That's up to you and how hungry you are.

If your children see you eating appropriate portions of all the food groups,
they will do it too. So being a good role model benefits everyone!

**Use the measurement tools you've got on your own body to help
inform your portion sizes and show your littles how they can too!**

HOW TO USE THIS BOOK

Combining you and your little's favorite Mother Goose rhyme with spending time in the kitchen is the whole purpose of this book. So that's where you should start: reading the rhymes together. Look at the pictures and talk about what you see. What looks good to eat? Read the ingredients and the instructions aloud, too. Your child will learn new vocabulary words related to food and cooking. And hearing your voice will connect the nourishment of the recipe to the activity you'll do with your child.

STARTS WITH:

Reading the nursery rhyme with your little one.

FOLLOWED BY:

Delicious recipes that bring the rhyme to your table.

INCLUDES:

Essential information on how to go about feeding your family with tips on how to involve kids.

BONUS:

Encourages imagination, exploration, personalization, discovery of language, foods and fine motor skills—**ALL** things that support your kids' development.

HOW TO USE THIS BOOK

MOUTH WATERING FOOD PHOTOS

NUTRITIONAL BENEFIT

NUTRITION NIBBLE Which flowers are edible? Well, here are just a few colorful and edible flowers you can add to your recipes: Borage blossoms, Calendula, Violets Zucchini blossoms, Hibiscus, Lavender, Nasturtiums, Pansies, Roses and Sage flowers.

RECIPE TITLE

RECIPE YIELD, ALLERGY INFO AND DIET RESTRICTIONS

CHALLENGE LEVEL AND COOKING TIMES

FLOWER ICE

Makes: 1 tray of ice cubes

Contains: None of the Common Allergens

Diet Type: Gluten Free, Dairy Free

Challenge Level: Piece of Cake

Active Time: 10 minutes

Total Time: 1 hour (depending on freeze time)

Like Jack and Jill, your little needs to fetch a pail of water to make this recipe.

INGREDIENTS

- 1 packet edible flowers
  (*Tip*: Just because you can eat these flowers doesn't mean you have to. We usually discard the flowers once the ice melts.)
- Filtered water

  Note: For this recipe you need an ice cube tray. We like silicone trays best.

KIDS CAN

- Do this whole process!

WATCH OUT FOR

- Tiny water spills
- Impatience while water freezes into ice

KIDS CAN DO THESE

THESE REQUIRE A WATCHFUL EYE

INSTRUCTIONS

1. Fill an ice cube mold to the half-way point with purified water.
2. Place 1 or 2 edible flowers or flower petals in each mold.
3. Freeze for 15 minutes or until ice starts to take hold of the flower (flowers float) to keep it in place.
4. Fill the remaining space in the ice cube molds with more filtered water. Return to freezer.
5. Once frozen, you can pull out these ice cubes on a hot day and add to your favorite cold drinks.

RECIPE INGREDIENTS AND INSTRUCTIONS

MOTHER GOOSE MIX UP   Add edible flowers to your popsicles, too! Follow the steps but replace water with 100% juice, or a mix of juice and water for a tasty and pretty treat. For a flavorful twist, instead of flowers, place a few fresh herb leaves in each ice cube mold.

223

A MIX UP IS A RECIPE VARIATION, BUT ITS TOTALLY UP TO YOU!

SOME PHRASES AND TERMS YOU'LL FIND

GLUTEN, DAIRY AND OTHER ALLERGENS

When applicable, I indicate if the recipe is gluten free, dairy free or contains any of the eight most common food allergens.

Gluten Free: Ingredients in the recipe are free from wheat, barley and rye. If a recipe includes oats, which can be cross-contaminated with gluten, I specify to buy certified gluten-free oats. For families following a gluten-free diet, please always check food labels thoroughly as even some additives can contain gluten.

Dairy Free: Ingredients in the recipe are free from milk or animal-milk products such as butter, sour cream, yogurt or cheese. These recipes may include dairy-free alternatives such as almond milk, soy milk or oil.

Contains Common Food Allergies: Ingredients in the recipe contain one or more of the eight common allergens. True food allergies are rare, but some foods are more likely to cause an allergic reaction than others. These eight foods cause around 90% of food allergies:

Milk	*Wheat*	*Tree Nuts*	*Shellfish*
Egg	*Fish*	*Peanuts*	*Soy*

For the convenience of the parent and safety of the child, I note when a recipe contains any of the eight most common allergens. Recipes that do not contain any of the eight common allergens will say: **Contains:** None of the Common Allergens.

If your child does not have a known allergy, there is no reason to avoid these foods.

SOME PHRASES AND TERMS YOU'LL FIND

CHALLENGE LEVEL

This indicates how much work is involved in making the recipe. There are three different categories.

Piece of Cake. This refers to easy recipes that are straightforward and forgiving. Sometimes they have quite a few steps but don't require a lot of experience.

Just a Pinch Involved. These are medium-easy recipes that require a bit more attention but often sound harder than they are. Once you make them a couple of times, they're a cinch.

So Worth the Effort. These recipes require some cooking experience but aren't hard *per se*. They are simply more involved. These are the types of recipes that will pay back in spades.

TIME

Active Time: The amount of time you'll be preparing and focused on cooking.
Total Time: The active time plus the passive time marinating, resting, baking, freezing, waiting for yeast to rise, etc.—this is the start to finish time.

NUTRITION NIBBLE

The "shout out" to why you should feel good about feeding this dish to your family. While all food has a place at your table, Nutrition Nibbles draw your attention to particularly valuable nutrition info or dietary advice. Creating balanced nutrition is about more than what we eat, so sometimes Nutrition Nibbles will explain strategies to support your child's journey of food discovery and acceptance.

MOTHER GOOSE MIX UP

Recipes are all about personalization. In the Mother Goose Mix Up, I share suggestions on ways to add a twist, but, please, don't be limited by my ideas. Get creative. You and your little may discover something new and create a family classic!

KIDS CAN

WATCH OUT FOR

KIDS CAN

My favorite section! Here you'll find a short list of actionable tasks your child can do to get involved. These tasks are safe, engaging and fun. Kids can pop in and help and then go play. Or they can stay and 'supervise' your cooking from start to finish.

Remind children to wash their hands before and after preparing food, to wash vegetables and fruit before eating and not to mix ready-to-eat foods with foods that need to be cooked.

WATCH OUT FOR

Here is where I alert Mom and Dad about kitchen tools or processes that require a watchful eye. For example, hot surfaces and sharp knives. This section helps you, the adults, pay attention to potential hazards so you can avoid them. Getting burned or cut puts an end to the fun fast!

TIPS

Years of cooking, talking and teaching have taught me a thing or two about shortcuts that work and what other people I admire do to make life easier in the kitchen. I happily share these with you.

SETTING THE TABLE

Kids who aren't ready to cook can still help!

We always need someone to help set the table. For detailed instructions on table setting, and other activities, see **Chapter 4 - Crafty Additions**.

When you make something really tasty from this book, please share a photo or story with me. You can email me at mothergoose@storybooknutrition.com or tag @storybooknutrition on Instagram. With your permission, I'll share your accomplishments with others on my social media so everyone can enjoy and benefit from your "aha moment"!

SOME PHRASES AND TERMS YOU'LL FIND

COOKING "LACEY-ISMS" IN THIS BOOK

Blow-on-it-hot: The hottest temperature your mouth can stand. Some foods taste better fresh out of the pot or pan. Blow on each bite, test with your tongue and eat as soon as it is cool enough for you.

Handful: The amount of food (herbs, leafy greens, nuts or chocolate chips) that a child or parent can grab with one hand. It is generally expected to be ¼ to ½ cup.

Lick-the-spoon-clean: So delicious, you need to get every last bit—by any means possible... even if it includes licking the spoon!

Spoon Test: Coat the back of a spoon with a sauce and run your finger through it. If your finger leaves a path, the sauce, glaze or curd is ready.

Straight-from-the-fridge-cold: the temperature of an ingredient, like butter, when it comes out of the refrigerator, about 35°F to 38°F.

Toothpick Test: To see if your baked item is ready to come out of the oven, insert a toothpick into the center of the deepest section. If the toothpick comes out clean or with only a few crumbs, remove the dish from the oven and set it on a cooling rack. If the toothpick comes out with wet dough stuck to it, reset the timer and bake longer. Use the Toothpick Test when baking cakes, muffins, breads and cookies.

COOKING ASSUMPTIONS

In this book, you can always assume the following	
Eggs	Always large
Juice of a lemon	2 tablespoons of juice
Zest of a lemon	1 tablespoon of zest
1 garlic clove minced	1 teaspoon of fresh minced garlic (Or ¼ teaspoon powdered garlic)
Stick of butter (unsalted)	8 tablespoons or 115 grams
Tablespoon	Approximately 15 milliliters (mL)
Teaspoon	Approximately 5 milliliters (mL)
Baking	Always convection bake setting

UTENSILS: WHAT YOU'LL NEED

I've moved my kitchen halfway around the world and back again. Out of necessity and opportunity, I've streamlined my equipment and don't have a lot of fancy gadgets or gizmos. But the ones I have kept, I consider to be my "other babies."

For some, this portfolio of kitchen accessories may be aspirational, while others will notice that my equipment isn't as nice as theirs. These tools are useful to have, but don't feel like you have to run out and buy new devices. Just use 'em if you got 'em. And please know that no matter what you've got in your kitchen, you can still prepare delicious foods without expensive gadgets. While it may be faster to chop using a food processor, you can always cut food by hand with a good knife. And while there are lots of options for adults based on your personal preference, I do suggest getting the kid-friendly tools (flagged in green) to keep cooking safe and fun for the littles.

Whether you're setting up a kitchen for the first time or simply want to do more cooking, having the basic gear for you and your child is an essential part of success.

Apple Corer

Blender

Box Grater

Bread Pan / Casserole Dish

Cake Frosting Scraper

Cake Pans (2 x 6 inch)

Cake Turntable

Cast Iron Skillet

Cheesecloth

Chef's Knife for Kids

Cocottes

Cooling Rack

Cutting Boards

Digital Infrared Thermometer

Food Processor

Frosting Spatula

Garlic Twister

Icing Bag and Tips

Kid-Safe Scissors

Kids Apron

Kitchen Mechanical Timer

Kitchen Scale

Lemon squeezer

Measuring Cups

Measuring Spoons

Mesh Strainer

Mixing Bowl

Mortar and Pestle

Muffin Tin

Nonstick Frying Pan

Pie Plate

Rolling Pin

Rubber Spatula / Scraper

Salad Spinner

Saucepan

Serving Spoons

Sheet pans in various sizes

Sifter

Silicone Baking Mat

Silicone Brush

Silicone Gummy Bear Mold

Silpat

Slow Cooker

Spiralizer

Spring Form Pans

Stand-Up Mixer

Stockpot

Strainer / Colander

Vegetable Brush

Vegetable Peeler

Wavy Chopper Cutter

Whisk

Wide, Deep Pot

Wire Mesh Spider

Wok

Zester / Microblade

Phone, notebook, pens and sticky pads to take pictures, make notes and call friends to come over and eat!

TIME TO GET STARTED

Now, you know all you need to get started *Celebrating with Mother Goose*!

Just a quick word about the recipes you're about to prepare. The title and page number of every nursery rhyme are highlighted in ***bold italic*** so you can read the inspiration for each recipe before you make it.

I've organized the recipes into sections that make sense for the way my family eats but don't be intimidated by a label. Many recipes fit into more than one category, and hey, if you want **Grilled Cheese** for breakfast and a **Crumble Bar** for dessert, go for it. A quick head's up, Chapter 5 is dedicated to parents—it's not for kids—because we deserve a little somethin' too!

The only rules when it comes to what you eat and when are the rules you make...

No judgments here. Just enjoy!

CHAPTER ONE
SIT DOWN SNACKS   44

CHAPTER TWO
DULCES AND DESSERTS — 120

Cherry on Top ***169***
Cherry On Top Thumbprint Cookies 171

Little Miss Muffet ***173***
Poppy Seed Crepes with Lemon Curd 175

Curdy, Curdy Custard ***179***
Hazelnut Tapioca Custard 181

Upstairs, Downstairs ***183***
Spiced Apple Cream Pot 185

Ice Cream, A Penny A Lump ***187***
Mango Lime Cannoli Cones 189

CHAPTER THREE
DRINKS TO SIP 190

Strawberries in the Sea 193
Classic Agua de Piña 195
Virgin White Grape Sangria 197
Cucumber and Raspberry Refresher 199
Halloween Mocktail 201
Green Dream 203
Pineapple Basilade 205
Mote Con Huesillos 207
Virgin Moscow Mule 209

CHAPTER FOUR
CRAFTY ADDITIONS 210

Hey Diddle Diddle ***213***
Set the Table 215

Blow Wind, Blow ***217***
Blow Wind Blow Gluten-Free Flour Blend 219

CHAPTER FIVE
MOTHER GOOSE CUTS LOOSE   240

CHAPTER 1

Sit Down Snacks

As a nutritionist and mom—there's a lot of pressure around snacks. Trying to keep blood sugar levels under control while serving tasty and convenient options, is no simple feat when tummies are grumbling. Keep in mind, you can always serve up leftovers because a "snack" is really just a smaller portion of a regular meal. Still, I know sometimes we need proper snack food. I've got you covered.

This chapter encompasses all kinds of foods, from lunchbox-worthy fare to foods you can serve for dinner (hello, crab cakes!). Don't take this as an invitation to graze without intention though. Instead, "sit down snacks" should be a designated time for you and your littles to refuel between family meals.

Our active kids need to re-up their nutrition and energy every two to four hours. So, go ahead and eat a little or a lot from this collection of savory and sweet snacks!

P.S. All the recipes in this chapter make terrific party-food for celebrations.

ROBERT ROLEY

ROBERT ROLEY

Robert Roley rolled around
Roll round,
A round roll Robert Roley rolled
Round;
Where rolled the round roll
Robert Roley rolled around?

ROCK YOUR WORLD SNACKS

When snack time "rolls around" in your home, keep these
fresh, homemade treats in mind. They're fun to prepare
together and encourage healthy snacking to keep you and
your littles from watching the clock until dinner.

NUTRITION NIBBLE Kale is high in nutrients and low in calories, making these chips one of the most nutrient-dense snacks you can eat.

KALE CHIPS

Makes: 12 handfuls (about 3 cups)
Contains: None of the Common Allergens
Diet Type: Gluten Free, Dairy Free

Challenge Level: Piece of Cake
Active Time: 30 minutes
Total Time: 30 minutes

INGREDIENTS

- Large bundle (6½ ounces) of curly green or purple kale
- 2 tablespoons extra virgin olive oil
- Seasonings of choice (pinch of sea salt, black pepper, cumin powder, chili powder, garam masala or nutritional yeast, whatever you fancy.)

KIDS CAN

- Wash and spin kale
- Massage leaves with olive oil and seasonings
- Taste test chips (parents, make sure chips aren't too hot)

WATCH OUT FOR

- Hot oven door and pans

INSTRUCTIONS

1. Preheat oven to 300°F, convection bake.
2. Rinse and thoroughly dry kale then tear leaves into pieces. Discard thick ribs and stems.
   (***Tip:*** *Don't just trim the stems below the leaves. Remove most of the stem from the center of the leaf, where it acts like a supporting rib.*)
3. Place a silpat or parchment paper on top of a baking sheet (you need two sheets).
4. Dump the kale onto the prepared baking sheet and pour olive oil on top.
5. Sprinkle leaves with salt and pepper and other spices as desired. Use your hands to massage the leaves and distribute the oil and seasonings evenly.
6. Spread kale over the baking sheets, don't let the individual kale leaves touch so they crisp while baking.
7. Bake for 10 minutes, then take out a test chip. Kale chips should be crispy and very slightly golden brown. If the kale is still chewy, turn the pans around and flip the leaves over with rubber tongs to ensure an even crispiness. Bake 2 minutes more. Watch closely, as chips can burn easily.
8. Remove from oven and let cool slightly. Chips will crisp up even more once out of the oven.
9. Enjoy chips blow-on-it-hot! Kale chips are best fresh.

NUTRITION NIBBLE A few handfuls of crispy tortilla chips will give your littles the extra energy they need to stay happy until dinnertime. Let each child put some chips in a little bowl to keep portions appropriate and serve with **Easy Guacamole** (p. 53) or **Piña and Avocado Salsa** (p. 55) for an extra dose of fruits and vegetables.

HOMEMADE CORN TORTILLA CHIPS

Makes: About 100 chips

Contains: Peanuts (if using peanut oil)

Diet Type: Gluten Free, Dairy Free

Challenge Level: Piece of Cake

Active Time: 15 minutes

Total Time: 30 minutes

Wondering why you'd ever make chips when you can buy them at the store? One bite of these freshly fried corn tortilla chips and you'll never ask yourself that question again—they are that good, y'all.

INGREDIENTS

- 48 ounces (1½ quarts) peanut, vegetable or canola oil
- 16 fresh corn tortillas
- Salt to taste

KIDS CAN

- Use kid-safe scissors to cut tortillas into triangles (with supervision)

WATCH OUT FOR

- Hot oil can splatter
- Children should leave the kitchen while tortillas are frying

INSTRUCTIONS

1. Stack tortillas in groups of 4. Cut each stack into 6 triangle wedges each.
2. Heat the oil in a large wok or Dutch oven to 350°F. To test if oil is ready, place a small piece of tortilla in the pan. If the tortilla starts to bubble and fry, the oil is sufficiently hot. If not, wait a few minutes, test again, and then continue.
3. Add ⅓ of tortilla triangles and fry. Agitate and flip them constantly with a wire mesh spider until bubbles slow to a trickle and chips are pale golden brown. This takes about 2 minutes.
4. Transfer to a paper towel-lined bowl, season with salt, and toss.
5. Allow excess oil to drain off the chips for 30 seconds, then transfer to a second, dry bowl.
6. Repeat with remaining tortillas in 2 more batches. Serve blow-on-it-hot.

NUTRITION NIBBLE Creamy, soft and mild, avocados are the perfect fruit for beginner eaters and first-time cooks. Even the littlest little can mash the flesh. While my kids love to wash and pick the cilantro, they prefer to eat it on the side, instead of mixed into the dip. Repeated exposure to new foods like cilantro, and respecting kids' preferences (leaving it on the side) reduces picky eating and increases acceptance.

EASY GUACAMOLE

Makes: About 1 cup

Contains: None of the Common Allergens

Diet Type: Gluten Free, Dairy Free

Challenge Level: Piece of Cake

Active Time: 15 minutes

Total Time: 15 minutes

INGREDIENTS

- Juice of 1 lime
- 1 medium avocado
- Handful of cilantro
- Salt, pepper, cumin and garlic powder, to taste

KIDS CAN

- Roll and squeeze the lime
- Mash avocado
- Wash and spin cilantro
- Separate cilantro leaves from stems
- Stir

WATCH OUT FOR

- Sharp knives for cutting the lime and avocado

INSTRUCTIONS

1. Set lime on the table and roll it with the palm of your hand. This will loosen up the juices inside.
2. Cut avocado in half, remove pit, scoop out the flesh, and put it into a bowl.
   Mash the avocado with the back of a fork.
3. Squeeze in lime juice.
4. Wash and spin the cilantro. With your fingers, tear cilantro leaves from the stems and break into tiny pieces. Add to the avocado and lime.
5. Taste. Add salt, pepper, cumin and garlic powder as desired. Enjoy alone or with **Homemade Corn Tortilla Chips** on page 51.

NUTRITION NIBBLE   Pineapples contain a wide variety of vitamins, minerals and enzymes (like bromelain) that collectively help suppress inflammation. The high vitamin C content aids in the absorption of iron from the diet, so pair this salsa with animal protein for a double health benefit.

PIÑA ⟨AND⟩ AVOCADO SALSA

Makes: About 1 cup

Contains: None of the Common Allergens

Diet Type: Gluten Free, Dairy Free

Challenge Level: Piece of Cake

Active Time: 30 minutes

Total Time: 30 minutes

INGREDIENTS

- 1 ripe avocado
- 1 cup fresh or canned pineapple
- 1 green onion
- Juice of 1 lime, plus more to taste
- Handful of fresh cilantro
- Handful of coconut flakes, toasted

KIDS CAN

- Roll and squeeze the lime
- Chop avocado with help
- Wash and spin cilantro
- Separate cilantro leaves from stems
- Stir
- Learn the Spanish word for pineapple (piña)

WATCH OUT FOR

- Sharp knives for cutting the lime and avocado
- Tiny cuts on your hands will sting if lime juice gets inside

INSTRUCTIONS

1. Wash avocado. Cut the avocado in half, remove pit and scoop out the flesh.
   On a cutting board, chop avocado and pineapple into small cubes. Transfer to a medium bowl.
2. Mince green onion and add it to the bowl.
3. Squeeze in the lime juice.
4. Tear the leaves off the cilantro stems and rip them into smaller pieces
   (or cut leaves with kid-safe scissors).
5. Toast coconut flakes in a dry, nonstick frying pan until fragrant and light brown. Sprinkle on top just before serving.
6. Season with salt and pepper to taste.

NUTRITION NIBBLE Crab is a popular seafood with children and its soft, mild-tasting flesh is a rich source of lean protein, B12 and copper.

CRAB CAKES {WITH} REMOULADE SAUCE

Makes: 9 crab cakes

Contains: Milk, Egg, Wheat, Shellfish

Challenge Level: Just a Pinch Involved

Active Time: 45 minutes

Total Time: 1 hour

INGREDIENTS

- 1 pound frozen crab meat, defrosted, drained and picked over
- 4½ tablespoons unsalted butter, melted and cooled
- 4½ tablespoons green onion, chopped
- 1½ tablespoons parsley, finely chopped
- 1 teaspoon dried dill
- Juice and zest from 1 lemon
- 1 teaspoon salt
- 1½ teaspoon hot sauce (We like Frank's Red Hot Sauce), optional
- 3 eggs, lightly beaten
- 1 garlic clove, minced
- 2¼ cups panko, divided
- 4 tablespoons canola oil, divided

KIDS CAN

- Twist the garlic twister to mince garlic
- Set the table, wash hands and generally get ready for dinner. (This recipe is best left to grown ups).
- Make Remoulade Sauce

WATCH OUT FOR

- Hidden bits of crab shell in the meat, and hot oil spitting and splattering out of the pan

INSTRUCTIONS

1. Put the first 10 ingredients (up to and including the garlic) and 1¾ cups of the panko in a large bowl. Gently combine using your hands or a spoon.
2. Shape the crab meat mixture into nine rectangular patties (about the length of an adult's index finger, 2 fingers wide, and 1-inch thick).
3. Sprinkle the remaining ½ cup of panko on a large plate. Gently transfer the cakes to the plate, pressing the sides into the panko.
4. Cover and chill until slightly firm, about 15 minutes.
5. Heat 2 tablespoons of canola oil in a large nonstick skillet over medium-high heat. Place 3 crab cakes in the hot oil and cook until golden brown, about 4 minutes per side. Transfer to a wire rack set on top a baking sheet. (**Tip:** *Placing the wire rack over a baking sheet catches any drips and makes clean-up a breeze.*)
6. Repeat with the remaining oil and cakes. Serve immediately or store in an oven heated to 200°F for up to 10 minutes, while you set the table and generally get ready for dinner.

REMOULADE SAUCE

Makes: About 1 cup

Contains: Egg

Diet Type: Gluten Free, Dairy Free

Challenge Level: Piece of Cake

Active Time: 10 minutes

Total Time: 15 minutes

INGREDIENTS

- ¾ cup mayonnaise
- ¼ cup sweet pickle relish or chopped pickle
- 1 green onion, finely chopped
- 1 garlic clove, minced
- 2 tablespoons Creole mustard or whole grain mustard
- 1 tablespoon stone ground mustard
- 1 tablespoon hot sauce (We like Frank's Red Hot Sauce)
- 1 teaspoon lemon juice
- ½ teaspoon paprika
- Pinch of fresh cracked black pepper

KIDS CAN

- Measure, squeeze and stir ingredients

WATCH OUT FOR

- Strong-flavored ingredients and sharp knives
- Wash hands with soap and water after handling spices to avoid getting pepper in little eyes

INSTRUCTIONS

1. This one is easy! In a medium bowl, stir all ingredients together until well mixed. Serve with Crab Cakes or as a dipping sauce for seafood, fried food or vegetables.

MOTHER GOOSE MIX UP Some remoulade sauces are red and spicy. If you prefer that style, swap half the mayo for ketchup, add a splash of vinegar and taste. Adjust seasonings as necessary.

FRESH VEGGIE PLATE

WITH LEMON HUMMUS AND HONEY MUSTARD DIPPING SAUCE

Makes: 1 platter

Contains: None of the Common Allergens

Diet Type: Gluten Free, Dairy Free

Challenge Level: Piece of Cake

Active Time: 15 minutes

Total Time: 15 minutes

INGREDIENTS

These are just suggestions, you can put any veggies on the plate. Try a mix of favorites as well as new vegetables:

- Carrots
- Celery
- Baby tomatoes
- Mushrooms
- Bell peppers
- Asparagus
- Cauliflower
- Broccoli
- Olives, pickles or marinated veggies
- Leaves (spinach, basil, even iceberg lettuce)
- Zucchini or summer squash
- Cucumber

KIDS CAN

- Wash produce and pat dry
- Chop veggies into fun shapes with supervision. This is a perfect time to break out the Wavy Chopper Cutter and Chef's Knife for Kids

WATCH OUT FOR

- Slippery vegetables. Definitely assist kids as they chop with kid-friendly knives

INSTRUCTIONS

1. Cut a variety of whatever colorful vegetables (the more colors the better!) into different shapes and arrange them on a kid-friendly platter.
2. Whip up a couple of dips (I usually offer one sweeter dip like **Honey Mustard Dipping Sauce** (p. 62) and one with healthy fats and protein, like **Lemon Hummus** (p. 63) or **Easy Guacamole** (p. 53).
3. Put the platter where tiny hands can easily reach. Children can snack on plain veggies or dip in the sauces for a crunchy, fresh, delicious snack. (*Tip: If your kids turn their noses up at veggies, increase their "acceptance" by adding 1 or 2 cut-fruit options on the plate. They may go for the fruit first but eventually their little hands will wander to the veggies.*)

HONEY MUSTARD DIPPING SAUCE

Makes: About 6 tablespoons
Contains: Egg (in the mayo)
Diet Type: Gluten Free, Dairy Free

Challenge Level: Piece of Cake
Active Time: 5 minutes
Total Time: 5 minutes

INGREDIENTS

- 2 tablespoons local honey
- 2 tablespoons yellow mustard
  (We use French's mustard.)
- 2 tablespoons mayonnaise

KIDS CAN

- Do it all!

WATCH OUT FOR

- This recipe is pretty tame and straight forward—you should be fine

INSTRUCTIONS

1. This one is easy!
   Just scoop ingredients into a small bowl and stir until uniform in texture.
   Serve cold or room temperature.

LEMON HUMMUS

Makes: About 2 cups
Contains: None of the Common Allergens
Diet Type: Gluten Free, Dairy Free

Challenge Level: Piece of Cake
Active Time: 10 minutes
Total Time: 10 minutes

INGREDIENTS

- (1) 15-ounce can chickpeas, drained and rinsed
- 1 garlic clove, minced
- 2 tablespoons warm filtered water
- 2 tablespoons extra virgin olive oil
- 2 tablespoons tahini
- Juice of 1 lemon
- Salt and pepper to taste
- Ground paprika for garnish

KIDS CAN

- Twist the garlic twister to mince garlic
- Rinse and drain chickpeas
- Squeeze lemon

WATCH OUT FOR

- Sharp blades of the food processor

INSTRUCTIONS

1. This one is easy!
   Just combine all ingredients into your food processor or high powered blender and blitz
   until smooth and creamy. Garnish with fresh cracked pepper, paprika and a swirl of olive oil.

NUTRITION NIBBLE Chickpeas (also known as garbanzo beans) add a blast of plant-based protein to your child's snack. The protein and fiber combination leave your child satisfied so they can last until dinner.

BUILD A SNACK DINNER

TURN YOUR VEGGIE PLATTER INTO DINNER IN JUST 4 EASY STEPS!

Sometimes all we need is a "snacky" kind of dinner. Follow the steps below to add a little "umph" to your veggie plate and make it a full meal!

~ STEP ONE ~

Start with the Fresh Veggie Plate with Lemon Hummus
and Honey Mustard Dipping Sauce as a base.

~ STEP TWO ~

Add some fruit: go for whatever fruit is in season
or used dried. Make sure to wash fresh fruit first!

~ STEP THREE ~

Pump up the protein: Choose at least one kind
of cheese and one or two lean proteins like
smoked salmon and cold, cooked chicken.
(**Tip:** *1 ounce of meat and cheese per person.*)

~ STEP FOUR ~

Finally, add nuts and olives for a touch of healthy
fats and a little crunch.

NUTRITION NIBBLE When you make snack bars from scratch you have a chance to include the best ingredients like real fruit and rolled oats. These bars feel like a treat but are packed with vitamins, minerals and antioxidants to power-up the afternoon!

CRUMBLE BARS

Makes:	20 bars	**Challenge Level:**	Just a Pinch Involved
Contains:	Milk, Wheat	**Active Time:**	30 minutes
Diet Type:	Gluten Free Option	**Total Time:**	1 hour

INGREDIENTS

For the Filling:

- 1 cup frozen passion fruit
- 1 banana, mashed to a purée
  (***Tip:*** *You can substitute with a banana, or banana mango blend baby food purée*)
- ¼ cup granulated sugar
- ¼ cup cornstarch
- Juice of ½ a lemon

For the Base and Crumble Layer:

- 1 to 1½ cups rolled oats
  (choose certified gluten-free oats)
- 1 to 1½ cups all-purpose flour
  (for gluten-free option use **Blow Wind Blow Gluten-Free Flour Blend** on page 219)
- Pinch of salt
- ⅔ cup unsalted butter, softened in the microwave
- 1 cup brown sugar

KIDS CAN

- Measure dry ingredients
- Pinch, pat, smear and crumble the filling and crumble layers

WATCH OUT FOR

- Hot oven door and pans

INSTRUCTIONS ON NEXT PAGE

MOTHER GOOSE MIX UP

For a new spin on this recipe, replace the passion fruit filling with a mixed berry filling: Place 1½ to 2 cups frozen mixed berries in a large strainer. Rinse them with warm water and let them drain for about 30 minutes. Transfer berries to a bowl and mix in ¼ cup of sugar, 2 tablespoons of cornstarch and the juice of ½ a lemon. Voila! Berry Crumble Bars!

CRUMBLE BARS CONTINUED

INSTRUCTIONS

Prepare the Filling:

1. Place passion fruit in a fine mesh strainer. Rinse with warm water. Set strainer over a bowl so the excess juice can drain, about 30 minutes. *(**Tip:** If you skip the draining step, your bars will be soggy. With the juice that collects in your bowl, make a **Halloween Mocktail** on page 201.)*

2. Transfer the passion fruit pulp and seeds to a bowl and mix in the rest of the filling ingredients.

3. Preheat oven to 325°F, convection bake. Make the base and crumble.

For the Base and Crumble:

4. In a medium bowl mix the oats, flour, salt and brown sugar.

5. Use fingers to cut in all the butter until you have a crumble (similar to a wet sand texture).

6. Prepare a square spring form pan with cooking spray and fit parchment paper to the bottom.

7. Use your hands or the back of a spoon to press about ⅔ of the crumble into the base in an even layer. Place in the oven and bake for 10 minutes.

8. While the base layer bakes, gently press the passion fruit filling again to strain excess juices.

9. Remove base layer from the oven and carefully smooth a generous layer of passion fruit filling on top. Then pinch, drop, sprinkle and otherwise cover the top of the passion fruit with the remaining crumble mix.

10. Return to oven and bake for 25 minutes. When the bars shrink or pull away from the sides of the pan they are ready.

11. Remove crumble bars from the oven and allow to cool for 10 minutes.

12. Open the spring form buckle and gently lift it from the base. Allow the crumble to cool completely before cutting into bars.

13. Store any remaining bars in an airtight container in the refrigerator. Bars are less crumbly when cold.

FRUIT-FILLED ICE CREAM CONES

Makes: 8 cones
Contains: Milk, Wheat

Challenge Level: Piece of Cake
Active Time: 15 minutes
Total Time: 45 minutes

INGREDIENTS

- 8 store-bought ice cream cones
- ½ cup dark chocolate or semi-chocolate chips
- 2 cups fresh fruit, cut

KIDS CAN

- Dip cones in chocolate
- Select and wash fruit
- Fill cones with bite-size pieces of fresh fruit

WATCH OUT FOR

- Burning fingers on melted chocolate and hot bowls (even microwave-safe ones can be hot to the touch).

INSTRUCTIONS

1. Heat dark chocolate in a microwave-safe bowl in 30 second bursts, stirring so it melts.
   Dip the mouth of each cone into the melted chocolate.
2. Place dipped cones on a baking sheet lined with parchment paper.
   Transfer the baking sheet to the refrigerator or freezer so chocolate can set.
3. While cones chill, wash and cut the fruit into bite-sized pieces.
4. Once cool, about 15 minutes later, fill cones with fruit.

MOTHER GOOSE MIX UP

Running short on time? Just fill store-bought cones with chopped fruit and skip the chocolate dip. Have some extra **Kook-A-Bear Fruit Gummies** (p. 113) lying around? Add them to your cones for an extra special treat. **Fruit-Filled Ice Cream Cones** are great for play dates and birthday parties.

ROSEMARY CRACKERS

ROSEMARY CRACKERS

Rosemary Crackers with Agua de Piña to drink,
These make the finest of snacks I do think;
When I'm grown up and can have what I please
I think I shall always insist upon these.
What do you choose when you're offered a treat?
When Mother Goose says, 'What would you like to eat?'
Is it olives or cheese or cinnamon toast?
It's rosemary crackers that I love the most!

WITH ALL THE STORE-BOUGHT CRACKER OPTIONS, YOU MAY BE TEMPTED TO SKIP THIS RECIPE. DON'T! THESE ROSEMARY CRACKERS ARE SUPER EASY AND SUPER YUM!

ROSEMARY CRACKERS

Makes: 24 crackers
Contains: Egg, Tree Nuts
Diet Type: Gluten Free, Dairy Free

Challenge Level: Just a Pinch Involved
Active Time: 30 minutes
Total Time: 45 minutes

INGREDIENTS

- 2 cups blanched almond flour
- ½ teaspoon fine-grain sea salt
- 1 tablespoon dried or fresh rosemary, chopped
- 1 ounce filtered water
- 1 egg
- 1 tablespoon extra virgin olive oil

KIDS CAN

- Search for the ingredients
- Crack the egg
- Roll the dough
- Set the timer

WATCH OUT FOR

- Hot oven

INSTRUCTIONS

1. Preheat oven to 350°F, convection bake.
2. Combine almond flour, salt and rosemary in a medium mixing bowl.
3. Make a well in the center of the dry ingredients.
4. Add water, egg and olive oil to your well. Gently mix wet ingredients together until combined.
5. Slowly pull in the dry ingredients until dough forms. Dough will be tacky to the touch.
6. Place dough between 2 sheets of parchment paper and roll it out to an even thickness of about ⅛ inch. (**Tip:** *Instead of using two layers of parchment paper, you can place the cracker dough onto a silpat. Cover the dough with a sheet of parchment paper and roll over that.*)
7. Dust the raw cracker dough with sea salt and gently roll over it with the rolling pin to press in. Remove top layer of parchment paper and discard.
8. Place base layer of parchment paper or silpat on baking sheet and use a knife or pizza cutter to trim the dough into a large rectangle.
9. Cut into rectangular crackers, about 2 x 3 inches. (**Tip:** *Don't toss the trimmings, these "extras" are delish so we leave them on the pan to bake*).
10. Bake for 10 minutes.
11. Turn off the oven and let crackers sit inside the oven for an additional 10 minutes or until golden.
12. Enjoy. Leftovers can be stored in an airtight container on the counter.

HOCUS POCUS

HOCUS POCUS

Hocus Pocus!

Alakazam!

Abracadabra!

I think you can

Use *Please* and *Thank You,*

These words too,

Just like magic

Make wishes come true!

NUTRITION NIBBLE Hippocrates, considered by many to be the father of Western medicine, and famous for saying, "let food be thy medicine and medicine be thy food," prescribed garlic to his patients in Ancient Greece. Today we use garlic for its taste, but back in ancient times, garlic was considered a medicine – and science has now proven its beneficial properties. It is rich in vitamin C, vitamin B6 and manganese and high in brain-protective antioxidants.

GARLIC AND HERB MARINATED OLIVES

Makes: 2 jars

Contains: Milk

Diet Type: Gluten Free

Challenge Level: Piece of Cake

Active Time: 30 minutes

Total Time: 3 hours (includes 2 hours refrigeration)

I traveled to Tuscany and Umbria to study nutrition and the Mediterranean Diet as a graduate student back in 2013. Tuscans make food with only a few ingredients but they use the absolute best quality of what they can find. I encourage you to do the same. These garlic and herb marinated olives take me back to a summer of al fresco dining with professors and fellow students at long wooden tables.

INGREDIENTS

- ¾ cup extra virgin olive oil
- 10 garlic cloves, peeled and minced
- Zest and juice of 1 lemon
- 2 cups of big, green olives
- 2 cups Kalamata or purple olives
- 2 tablespoons fresh parsley, minced
- 2 sprigs (1½ tablespoons) fresh rosemary, minced
- Pinch red pepper flakes
- 6 ounces (200 grams) creamy Havarti, cubed

KIDS CAN

- Count garlic cloves
- Pick fresh herbs
- Scoop olives
- Squeeze the lemon
- Close the jar lid

WATCH OUT FOR

- Hot oil
- Red pepper flakes are spicy

INSTRUCTIONS

1. Infuse the olive oil. Combine oil and garlic in a small saucepan over medium-low heat. Cook, stirring gently, until garlic softens and begins to brown, about 15 minutes.
2. Set garlic-infused oil aside to cool to room temperature, about 20 minutes.
3. Meanwhile, zest and juice the lemon, and combine all the ingredients in a large resealable plastic bag.
4. When oil is cool, strain over a fine mesh colander and discard the garlic. Add it to the bag with the herbs, olives and cheese.
5. Refrigerate for 2 hours – the longer the better really. Transfer to pretty jars for storage. Toast some fresh bread (**Note:** bread is not gluten free) and serve along with toothpicks, salami, prosciutto, nuts and dried and fresh fruit.

ONION HEAD

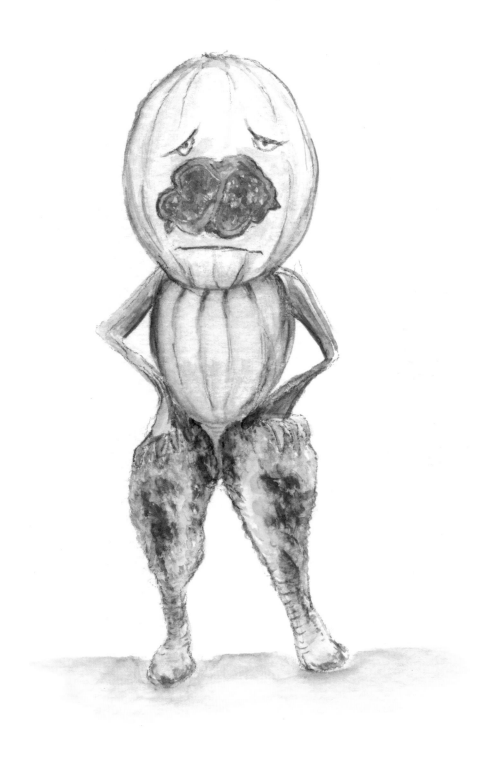

ONION HEAD

_____'s got a bunion

(Example: Axel's got a bunion -
Insert your child's name above)

A face like a pickled onion,

A nose like a squashed tomato

And legs like drumsticks.

NUTRITION NIBBLE Any time you can add vegetables to your kid's day you probably should. This salsa won't make you cry, despite having onions. In fact, it's an excellent introduction to onions, which are a natural antihistamine. So long allergies!

PEBRE

Makes: 4 cups

Contains: None of the Common Allergens

Diet Type: Gluten Free, Dairy Free

Challenge Level: Piece of Cake

Active Time: 20 minutes

Total Time: 30 minutes

Pebre is a fresh tomato, onion and herb salsa served with bread baskets on tables throughout Chile. Locals spread pebre instead of butter on their bread. My kids have learned to do the same. When Pebre is puréed it is called Chancho en Piedra, or "pig in stone." That's because it was hand ground by mortar and pestle—in "the good old days" before immersion blenders. Pebre isn't limited to dinner rolls; use it on top of grilled sausages, to flavor soups, or to liven up tacos.

INGREDIENTS

- 4 large, ripe tomatoes, diced and seeded
- ½ purple onion, diced
- 2 aji verde (green chili pepper), seeded and diced
- ⅔ bunch (3 handfuls) of cilantro or parsley, finely chopped
- Juice of 2 lemons
- 3 tablespoons vegetable oil
- Pinch of salt

KIDS CAN

- Wash produce and pat dry
- Wash and spin cilantro
- Separate cilantro leaves from stems

WATCH OUT FOR

- Sharp knives

INSTRUCTIONS

1. Wash the tomatoes, onion and aji verde pepper. Pat dry.
2. Wash and spin the cilantro then separate the leaves from the stems. Chop the leaves.
3. Finely chop the onion, and let it rest in cold water while you chop the rest of the ingredients.
4. Drain the onion and add it and the chopped veggies to a bowl for pebre.
   (**Tip:** *If you want to make chancho en piedra, blitz the salsa with an immersion blender until smooth.*)
5. Add the lemon juice, oil and salt to taste.
6. Serve cold or room temperature with warm bread.
7. Store extra pebre in an airtight container in the refrigerator.

GOLDILOCKS

GOLDILOCKS

When Goldilocks went to the house of the bears,

Oh what did her blue eyes see?

A bowl that was huge,

And a bowl that was small,

A bowl that was tiny and that was all,

And she counted them one, two, three,

She counted them one, two, three.

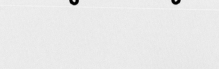

JUST RIGHT DIPS

These no-cook, cheesy and herby dips transform crudités and
sandwiches from ho-hum to lick-the-spoon-clean awesome.

Goldilocks went from bowl to bowl looking for one that was just right,
I think you'll find you can't "bear" to choose just one either.

SOUTHERN-STYLE
PIMENTO CHEESE

GREEN
SAUCE

CREAMY
CHIVE DIP

SOUTHERN-STYLE PIMENTO CHEESE (HUGE BOWL)

Makes: 4 cups
Contains: Milk
Diet Type: Gluten Free Option

Challenge Level: Piece of Cake
Active Time: 20 minutes
Total Time: 30 minutes

INGREDIENTS

- 4 ounce jar diced pimiento, drained
- ½ cup mayonnaise
- ½ cup cream cheese
- ½ cup sour cream
- Splash of Worcestershire sauce (For a gluten-free option, use Lea and Perrins)
- 1 teaspoon onion powder
- 1 teaspoon garlic powder
- Dash of your favorite hot sauce (We like Frank's Red Hot Sauce), plus more to taste
- 8 ounces medium yellow cheddar, grated
- 8 ounces sharp yellow cheddar, grated
- Freshly cracked black pepper

KIDS CAN

- Drain the pimiento
- Measure spices
- Splash Worcestershire sauce
- Grate cheese with supervision
- Stir and mix

WATCH OUT FOR

- Blades of the grater are sharp

INSTRUCTIONS

1. In a big bowl with lots of room, stir all ingredients except the cheese and black pepper together.
2. Incorporate the cheddar cheeses one handful at a time until all cheese is coated.
3. Top with fresh ground black pepper.
4. Cover and refrigerate for 20 minutes before serving.
5. Serve with crudités and crackers or store for up to one week in an airtight container.

MOTHER GOOSE MIX UP Use the pimento cheese dip to make tea sandwiches (see **Pimento Cheese Sandwiches** p. 97) or use as a unique substitute filling for my **Grilled Cheese Sandwiches** (p. 101)

GREEN SAUCE (SMALL BOWL)

Makes: About 1 cup

Contains: None of the Common Allergens

Diet Type: Gluten Free, Dairy Free

Challenge Level: Piece of Cake

Active Time: 15 minutes

Total Time: 15 minutes

INGREDIENTS

- 2 cloves garlic, chopped
- 1 cup parsley
- 1 cup cilantro
- ¼ cup fresh lemon juice
- ½ teaspoon salt
- 1 teaspoon ground coriander
- 1 teaspoon cumin
- 1 aji verde or mild green pepper, chopped (optional)
- ¼ cup extra virgin olive oil

KIDS CAN

- Wash herbs and spin dry
- Separate herbs leaves from stems
- Add ingredients to food processor

WATCH OUT FOR

- Sharp blades of the food processor

INSTRUCTIONS

1. Wash herbs and spin dry. Pick leaves from stems.
2. In a food processor, pulse all the ingredients except the olive oil.
3. Slowly pour in olive oil to the food processor as it runs. Stop when sauce is well combined.
4. Taste for seasoning and adjust if necessary.

NUTRITION NIBBLE Using fresh herbs like cilantro and parsley, is a great way to add flavor to your food without adding salt or fat.

CREAMY CHIVE DIP (TINY BOWL)

Makes: About 1 cup
Contains: Milk
Diet Type: Gluten Free

Challenge Level: Piece of Cake
Active Time: 10 minutes
Total Time: 10 minutes

INGREDIENTS

- 8 ounces queso fresco
- 2 handfuls (½ cup) chopped chives
- 3 to 4 tablespoons plain Greek yogurt
- ½ teaspoon onion powder or to taste
- Squeeze of lemon, optional

KIDS CAN

- Wash and dry chives
- Cut or tear chives and cheese
- Push the "on" button of the food processor with supervision

WATCH OUT FOR

- Sharp blades of the food processor

INSTRUCTIONS

1. Wash chives and pat dry.
2. Cut chives into small pieces with kid-safe scissors.
3. Open queso fresco and drain the liquid.
4. Tear or cut cheese into pieces (**Tip:** *You can use kid-safe scissors for this too.)*
5. Add chives, queso fresco and yogurt to a food processor. Pulse until smooth.
6. Taste, add lemon juice or onion powder if desired (We like it plain.).
7. Serve in a tiny bowl as a dip or use as a spread for sandwiches.

POLLY PUT THE KETTLE ON

POLLY PUT THE KETTLE ON

Polly, put the kettle on,
Polly, put the kettle on,
Polly, put the kettle on,
   We'll all have tea.

Sukey, take it off again,
Sukey, take it off again,
Sukey, take it off again,
   They've all gone away.

Blow the fire and make the toast,
Put the muffins on to roast,
Blow the fire and make the toast,
We'll all have tea.

TEA PARTY SANDWICHES

Tea time begins with tea sandwiches and ends with cakes
(see **Tea Party Sweets** starting on p. 139). Tea sandwiches are little three-bite
finger sandwiches that help tide us over between lunch and dinner. The cucumber
and egg salad versions are classics, while the chicken salad and pimento cheese
sandwiches are inspired by my life growing up in the American South.

TEA PARTY SANDWICHES

CHICKEN SALAD SANDWICHES

Makes: 24 tea sandwiches
Contains: Wheat, Tree Nuts
Diet Type: Dairy Free

Challenge Level: Piece of Cake
Active Time: 1 hour
Total Time: 1 hour 15 minutes

INGREDIENTS

- Up to 1 cup mayonnaise
- 1 teaspoon Dijon mustard
- ½ teaspoon granulated sugar
- Juice of 1 lemon
- Salt and pepper to taste
- 5 cups cooked chicken, shredded (**Tip:** *I use white meat from a rotisserie chicken or 2 large chicken breasts boiled and shredded—see below to learn how to boil a chicken.*)
- 3 small celery ribs, finely chopped
- ¾ cup parsley, finely chopped
- 2 cups green grapes, cut in half
- 3 green onions, sliced thin
- 2 handfuls (½ cup) sliced or slivered almonds
- 16 slices of your favorite sandwich bread, crusts removed

KIDS CAN

- Shred chicken
- Squeeze lemon
- Trim crusts from bread
- Grab handfuls of slivered almonds
- Taste test grapes, almonds and celery

WATCH OUT FOR

- Sharp knives
- Hungry neighbors! Just kidding, the more the merrier!

INSTRUCTIONS

1. In a large bowl, stir together mayonnaise, mustard, sugar, lemon juice, salt and pepper. Set aside.
2. Stir in chicken, celery, parsley, onion, grapes and almonds.
3. Let salad sit for 30 minutes so the flavors marry.
4. Spread 2 to 3 tablespoons of chicken salad between sandwich bread.
5. Cut each sandwich into thirds. Repeat until you have 24 sandwiches.
6. Store leftover chicken salad in a resealable container in the refrigerator.

MOTHER GOOSE COOKING TIP If using frozen chicken breasts, bring a large pot of water to a boil. Add frozen, boneless, skinless chicken breasts. Cook for about 30 minutes or until the chicken is cooked through (smaller chicken breasts take less time). Discard water and set chicken on a cutting board. Prepare the rest of the ingredients while chicken cools. When the chicken is cool enough to handle, use two forks and shred the meat, or cut it into cubes with a sharp knife.

EGG SALAD SANDWICHES

Makes: 24 tea sandwiches

Contains: Egg, Wheat

Diet Type: Dairy Free

Challenge Level: Just a Pinch Involved

Active Time: 45 minutes

Total Time: 1 hour (15 minutes for hard boiled eggs to cool)

These recipes makes more salad than you need to fill sandwiches, but they are so popular in my house (and in my neighborhood) that I always make extra. Eat leftover salads over lettuce—or simply with a fork and share with the neighbors who are sure to drop by.

INGREDIENTS

- 9 eggs
- 1 tablespoon Dijon or yellow mustard
- ½ cup mayonnaise
- 2 green onions, minced
- 2 dashes white pepper
- 1 tablespoon pickle juice or sweet pickle relish
- Pinch of salt
- Pinch dried dill weed
- Juice of ½ a lemon
- Sprinkle of sweet paprika to taste
- 16 slices of your favorite sandwich bread, crusts removed

KIDS CAN

- Count eggs
- Prepare ice bath
- Peel hard boiled eggs

WATCH OUT FOR

- Hot stove, hot water and hot eggs

INSTRUCTIONS

For the Hard Boiled Eggs:

1. Place eggs in a wide pot and cover with 1 inch of cold water.
2. Bring to a boil, then reduce heat to low and simmer for 10 minutes.
3. While eggs cook, set out a large bowl with ice water and set a strainer in the sink.
4. Strain eggs under cold running water, then submerge the eggs in an ice bath to cool completely.
5. Once completely cool, make the egg salad.

For the Egg Salad:

6. Crack egg on the counter, roll gently between the countertop and your hand, and peel for egg salad.
7. Roughly chop eggs. Set aside.
8. In a large mixing bowl, stir together remaining ingredients.
9. Fold in the chopped eggs.
10. Spread 2 to 3 tablespoons of egg salad between thin-sliced sandwich bread.
11. Cut sandwich into thirds.

CUCUMBER <small>AND</small> RADISH SANDWICHES

Makes: 18 tea sandwiches
Contains: Milk, Wheat

Challenge Level: Just a Pinch Involved
Active Time: 45 minutes
Total Time: 45 minutes

INGREDIENTS

For the Sandwich:

- 1 to 2 large cucumbers with a uniform shape
- 1 cup Greek yogurt (or substitute ricotta cheese)
- 1 cup crumbled feta cheese
- 3 radishes, sliced thin
- 2 cloves garlic, minced
- Salt and pepper to taste
- Handful mint leaves, cut in chiffonade
- 12 pieces of your favorite thin-sliced sandwich bread, crusts removed

For the Vinaigrette (whisk in small bowl):

- 2 tablespoons extra virgin olive oil
- ½ teaspoon dried oregano
- 1 teaspoon red wine vinegar

KIDS CAN

- Wash produce and pat dry
- Stir yogurt-cheese spread
- Trim crusts

WATCH OUT FOR

- Sharp blades of the mandolin or vegetable peeler

INSTRUCTIONS

1. Slice the cucumbers and radishes lengthwise using a mandoline at ⅛ inch (2 mm) thickness or with a vegetable peeler. (**Tip:** *When you get to the seeds, rotate the cucumber and slice from the other side. Save the interior part of the cucumber for a yummy **Cucumber and Raspberry Refresher** on p. 199)*
2. Lay the sliced cucumbers on a plate lined with a paper towel to drain excess moisture.
3. In a medium bowl, mix together yogurt, feta cheese, garlic, mint, salt and pepper.
4. Between 2 pieces of thin-sliced sandwich bread, alternate layers of yogurt-cheese spread, cucumber slices, and radishes.
5. Serve with a garnish of fresh mint and vinaigrette.

PIMENTO CHEESE SANDWICHES

Makes: 24 tea sandwiches
Contains: Milk, Wheat

Challenge Level: Piece of Cake
Active Time: 30 minutes
Total Time: 30 minutes

INGREDIENTS

- 1½ cups **Southern-Style Pimento Cheese** (p. 87)
- 16 pieces of thin-sliced sandwich bread

KIDS CAN

- Count slices of bread
- Trim crusts
- Build sandwiches

WATCH OUT FOR

- Nothing! This is a safe and easy recipe

INSTRUCTIONS

1. Trim the crusts from the bread.
2. Spread 2 tablespoons of **Southern-Style Pimento Cheese** between thin-sliced sandwich bread.
3. Cut sandwich into thirds.

NUTRITION NIBBLE Parents sometimes forget to think of cheese as a health food, but cheese is a great source of calcium, fat and protein - nutrients that kids need to grow and develop. Cheese also contains vitamins A and B-12 and minerals zinc, phosphorus and riboflavin.

IF ALL THE WORLD WERE PAPER

IF ALL THE WORLD WERE PAPER

If all the world were paper,
And all the sea were ink,
If all the trees
Were bread and cheese,
What should we have to drink?

A grilled cheese sandwich is just a hot sandwich made of bread and cheese. So why has this humble snack captured the hearts of our children? It's because the 5th flavor *umami* (the other flavors are sweet, salty, bitter and sour) tickles our taste buds and makes us smile. It's hard to put into words just what umami tastes like, but take one bite of these classic and crazy grilled cheese sandwiches and you'll know that umami is just the flavor you're looking for!

Nutrition Nibble

Wondering how much dairy your child needs each day? Look no further for answers than to your little one herself! While too much can be quite filling, too little dairy robs your child of key nutrients. Below is the average number of servings of dairy children need at various ages. Provide a variety of sources for your little and remember one serving is equal to one cup of milk or yogurt or two slices of cheese.

- 1 to 2 year olds get 1 serving per day
- 2 to 3 year olds eat or drink 1½ servings
- 4-year olds and onwards can have 2 servings a day

CLASSIC ⟨AND⟩ "CRAZY" GRILLED CHEESE SANDWICHES

Makes: 1 sandwich

Contains: Milk, Wheat

Challenge Level: Piece of Cake

Active Time: 15 minutes

Total Time: 15 minutes

INGREDIENTS

- 1 tablespoon unsalted butter
- 2 slices bread
- 2 ounces cheese, sliced or grated
- Extra fillings as desired
  (See below for my favorite "crazy" combos)

Favorite "Crazy" Grilled Cheese:

- Gouda Cheese + Green Apple
- Brie + Cheddar + Dates (pits removed and chopped)
- Grated Cheddar + Grated Mozzarella
- Cheddar + Mozzarella + Sliced Tomato
- Monterey Jack + Cheddar + Mashed Avocado
- Cheddar + Caramelized Onions

KIDS CAN

- Find ingredients in the refrigerator and counter
- Choose cheese types and crazy combinations

WATCH OUT FOR

- Hot stove
- Hot cheese oozing out of their sandwich. Yum!

INSTRUCTIONS

1. Heat a griddle or frying pan to medium heat.
2. Put a tablespoon of butter on the griddle and place the bread on top of it, smearing it around so the butter spreads out.
3. Immediately add any non-cheese filling like apples, dates or avocado on the non-buttered side of the bread, if using. Top with cheese(s) and close sandwich.
4. Cook until golden, about 2 minutes.
5. Flip and cook the other side until cheese is melty and bread is golden brown, about 2 minutes more.
6. Slice in half or in thirds and serve blow-on-it-hot.

I HAD A LITTLE HEN

I HAD A LITTLE HEN

I had a little hen, the prettiest ever seen;

She washed me the dishes and kept the house clean;

She went to the mill to fetch me some flour,

She brought it home in less than an hour,

She baked me my bread, she brewed me my ale,

She sat by the fire and told many a fine tale.

While living in Chile, we had a lovely Italian family as neighbors. Angie, the mom, runs a cozy focaccia-only café called Mangi. (If you are ever in Santiago, Chile, take your family there!) Angie uses a specially imported flour to make her dough, which is carefully kneaded by hand. When we moved from Chile, I created this no-knead "cheater's focaccia" to satisfy our craving for Angie's crunchy-on-the-outside and chewy-on-the-inside bread. This focaccia tastes like the real thing but uses easy to find all-purpose flour and takes a fraction of the work. *Buon appetito!*

NUTRITION NIBBLE

Extra virgin olive oil is what makes focaccia so unbelievably delicious. Extra virgin olive oil is the highest quality olive oil available, extracted from the olive fruit without the use of any heat or chemicals. Cold pressing the olives protects the more than 30 various types of phenolic compounds in the oil that help protect the body against free radicals. (Free radicals are molecules that cause cell damage and contribute to disease and the aging process). A staple of the Mediterranean Diet, extra virgin olive oil adds to the texture as well as the flavor of the bread. I genuinely find that the secret to the best focaccia is using a great tasting extra virgin olive oil.

BLUEBERRY NO-KNEAD FOCACCIA

Makes: 1 sheet pan of focaccia
Contains: Milk, Wheat

Challenge Level: Piece of Cake
Active Time: 45 minutes
Total Time: 13 hours (includes overnight proofing)

INGREDIENTS

- 4 cups all-purpose flour
- 1 teaspoon dry yeast
- 1½ cups warm filtered water
  (Slightly warmer than room temperature is perfect)
- 2 teaspoons salt
- ¼ cup extra virgin olive oil, divided, plus more for hands
- 4 ounces blueberries
- 3 to 4 slices white cheese
  (We like manchego, Swiss or white cheddar)
- Handful fresh basil leaves, torn
- Sprinkle of flaked sea salt to finish

KIDS CAN

- Stir with the chopstick
- Oil baking pan
- Make dimples in the dough
- Press in toppings

WATCH OUT FOR

- Hot oven

INSTRUCTIONS

1. Mix together flour, yeast and 1 cup of the water. Stir with a chopstick until you have a uniform dough.
   (**Tip**: *Making dough with a chopstick, keeps the bread from getting too tough - plus it's fun for the littles*).
2. Add the remaining ½ cup water 1 tablespoon at a time as you may not need it all depending on the humidity levels where you live. When the dough comes together and is really soft, stop adding water.
3. Add salt and 1 tablespoon olive oil and continue to mix with a chopstick until incorporated.
4. Coat a large bowl with 1 teaspoon of olive oil, and set the dough inside. Then cover with plastic wrap and allow to rise for 10 to 12 hours (overnight) or until dough has more than doubled in size and is very bubbly. In warmer climates, this will take less time.
5. Preheat oven to 400°F. Generously coat a rimmed baking sheet with olive oil.
6. Oil your hands so they are slick, then gently lift the dough (it will be sticky) out of the bowl and spread it onto the baking sheet.
7. Create dimples on the surface of the dough with your fingers.
8. Drizzle dimpled dough with the rest of the olive oil like the Italians do.
9. Season with flaked sea salt.
10. Press in basil, cheese and fresh blueberries.
11. Bake for 25 minutes or until golden. Allow to cool before cutting into squares.

MISTY, MOISTY MORNING

MISTY, MOISTY MORNING

One misty, moisty morning,
When cloudy was the weather,
I chanced to meet an old man
Clothed all in leather.

He began to compliment,
And I began to grin;
How do you do, and how do you do?
And how do you do again?

This is one of my all-time favorite rhymes. For me it is a real tongue twister, which makes it fun to read out loud. When we get to the end of the verse we all start shaking each other's hands, crossing our arms across one another, and chanting, "how do you do, and how do you do, and how do you do again?"

NUTRITION NIBBLE

I wanted a healthier fruit roll-up or fruit snack that Axel and Rex could take to school. One without artificial colors, flavors or loads of extra sugar. When my efforts fell flat, I called up Rachael, a fellow mom (who also happens to be a Le Cordon Bleu trained Chef) and asked for some backup. And thus, our homemade fruit leathers were born. They're packed with whole fruit ingredients and have a chewy, just-sticky-enough texture that kids love. Edible proof that when moms come together, the results are great.

FRUIT LEATHERS

Makes: 12 roll ups

Contains: None of the Common Allergens

Diet Type: Gluten Free, Dairy Free

Challenge Level: So Worth the Effort

Active Time: 10 minutes

Total Time: 4 hours (your oven is acting like a dehydrator)

INGREDIENTS

For Berry Fruit Leathers:
- 1 cup strawberries
- 1 cup blueberries
- 1 to 2 tablespoons agave (to taste)
- 1 teaspoon vanilla bean paste

For Tropical Fruit Leathers:
- 1 cup mango purée
- 1 banana
- 2 tablespoons mandarin or orange juice

KIDS CAN

- Wash fruit and pat dry
- Spread purée
- Set the timer

WATCH OUT FOR

- Hot oven
- Forgetting you have something in the oven (been there)

INSTRUCTIONS

1. Combine all ingredients in a blender and blend until smooth.
2. Line a baking sheet with silpat or parchment paper.
3. Use a rubber spatula or the back of a spoon to spread purée in a thin, even layer on top.
4. Bake at 190°F for 4 hours or until dry. (**Tip:** *We tested this recipe in Rachael's dehydrator as well. It works, but the texture is better in the oven.*)
5. Let cool. Cut into strips and/or fun shapes, and eat.
6. Wrap extra fruit leathers in plastic wrap and store in an airtight container.

KOOKABURRA

KOOKABURRA

Kookaburra sits in the old gum tree.
Merry, merry king of the bush is he.
Laugh, Kookaburra,
Laugh, Kookaburra,
Gay your life must be.

Kookaburra sits in the old gum tree,
Eating all the gumdrops he can see.
Stop, Kookaburra,
Stop, Kookaburra,
Leave some there for me.

Kookaburra sits in the old gum tree,
Counting all the monkeys he can see.
Wait, Kookaburra.
Stop, Kookaburra.
That's not a monkey, that's me!

STRAWBERRY, PEACH, GRAPE, PEPPER JELLY! WHATEVER FRUIT PRESERVE YOUR FAMILY LOVES THE MOST CAN BE TRANSFORMED INTO A CUTE FRUIT SNACK!

NUTRITION NIBBLE Most store-bought fruit snacks are not much different than candy, full of corn syrup, artificial colors and artificial flavors. These little Kook-a-Bears give you the chewy sweetness of a gummy without all the junk.

KOOK-A-BEAR FRUIT GUMMIES

Makes: 100 gummies

Contains: None of the Common Allergens

Diet Type: Gluten Free, Dairy Free

Challenge Level: Piece of Cake

Active Time: 15 minutes

Total Time: 45 minutes

INGREDIENTS

- 4 tablespoons fresh-squeezed orange juice
- ⅓ cup fruit-sweetened fruit preserves
- 1 tablespoon plus 1 teaspoon unflavored gelatin

KIDS CAN

- Choose the fruit preserve
- Juice the orange
- Fill the bear mold

WATCH OUT FOR

- Hot stove
- Sticky fingers

INSTRUCTIONS

1. Juice an orange until you get enough fresh orange juice for the recipe (or use store-bought).
2. Blend fruit preserves and juice with an immersion blender.
3. Transfer to a saucepan on medium heat. Whisk and sprinkle the gelatin into juice-preserve blend.
4. When gelatin has dissolved and the mixture is transparent, turn off heat.
5. Place silicon gummy bear trays on a baking sheet to hold them steady and flat.
6. Use a dropper to fill each gummy bear.
7. Place baking sheet in the freezer to chill the bears.
8. Check on gummies in 20 to 30 minutes. They should be firm, if not, give them more time.
9. Remove from the trays. Best served cold.

MOTHER GOOSE MIX UP

Toss Kook-a-Bears in sour sanding (also called sour sugar) to turn these fruit snacks into sour candy. (**Note:** Sour sanding is a food ingredient that is used to impart a sour flavor, made from citric acid and sugar.)

HOT CROSS BUNS

HOT CROSS BUNS

Hot-cross buns!
Hot-cross buns!
One a penny, two a penny,
Hot-cross buns!

If you have no daughters,
Give them to your sons;
One a penny, two a penny,
Hot-cross buns!

NUTRITION NIBBLE

When you think of the word "carbohydrate," or "carb," the first image that might pop into your head may be a slice of bread. You're right! Carbohydrates, along with proteins and fats, are one of the three macronutrients our bodies need to function. Carbs are broken down by the body into simple sugars. These sugars circulate in the bloodstream and are used for energy. Children need carbs to stay alert and active throughout the day.

BRAIDED EGG BUNS

Makes:	10 buns	**Challenge Level:**	So Worth the Effort
Contains:	Egg, Wheat	**Active Time:**	1 hour
Diet Type:	Dairy Free	**Total Time:**	3 hours (includes 2 hours for proofing)

I used to think making homemade bread would be too hard for me. But my kids love "fancy bread"—and by fancy I mean they like croissants, brioche and the medialunas we find in bakeries all over Chile. Pushed into action by their passion, I decided to give "fancy" breadmaking a try. Turns out, it's easier than I thought! The kids love to participate and are eager to twist, twirl, pinch and poke this braided bun dough into fun shapes. Painting the egg wash on top calls out their inner artist and they approach each knot, silicone paint brush in hand, with the concentration of a master painter. The end result? Big smiles and a happy dance when they get to eat their masterpiece.

INGREDIENTS

For the Dough:
- 2¼ teaspoons active dry or instant yeast
- ¾ cup warm filtered water
- 4 tablespoons granulated sugar
- 3¾ cups all-purpose flour
- 1 teaspoon salt
- 2 eggs
- ⅓ cup vegetable oil

For the Egg Wash:
- 1 egg, lightly beaten with 1 tablespoon filtered water

KIDS CAN

- Divide the dough into 10 equal balls
- Roll dough into "snakes"
- Help fold and tie the dough into fun shapes
- Paint the knots with egg wash

WATCH OUT FOR

- Hot oven and oven door

INSTRUCTIONS ON NEXT PAGE

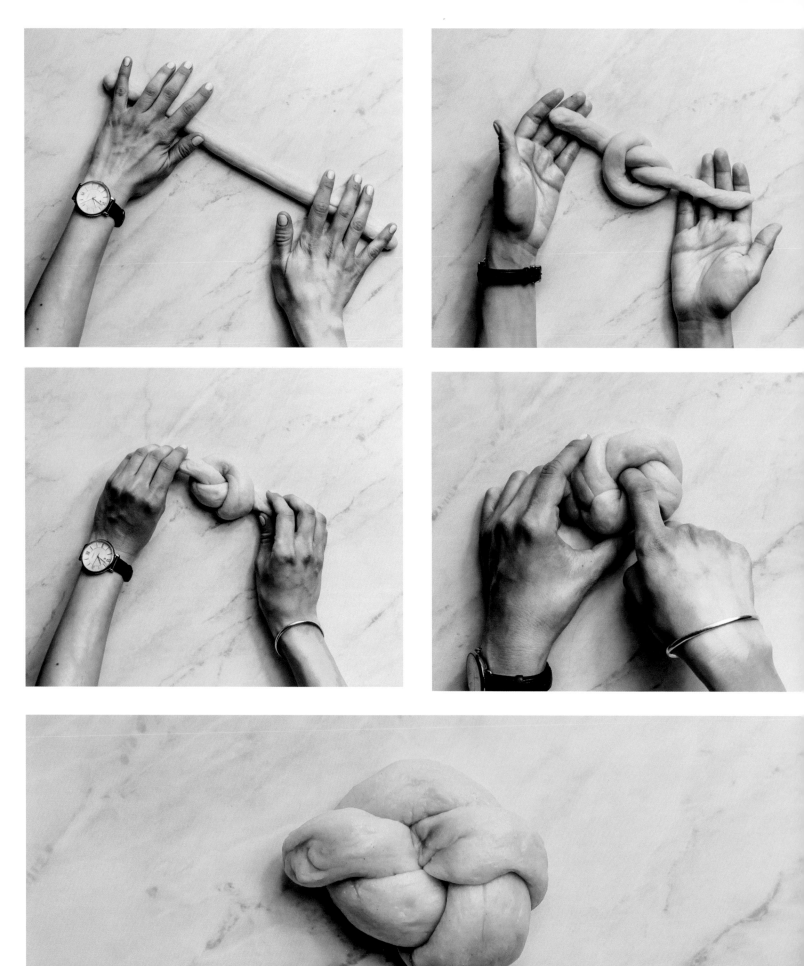

BRAIDED EGG BUNS CONTINUED

INSTRUCTIONS

1. In a large bowl or in your stand-up mixer, whisk together all the dry ingredients until combined.

2. Add warm water, eggs and oil to the above dry ingredient blend, then knead together or use hook attachment of stand-up mixer to work into a dough. (**Tip**: *If you have a stand-up mixer, use the hook attachment on low speed, which is level 4 or 6, depending on your mixer. Stop mixing when you have a dough ball.*)

3. Paint the interior of a large bowl with oil and place the dough ball inside, cover it with plastic wrap and let the dough sit at room temperature until it doubles in size, about 2 hours.

4. Line a baking sheet with parchment paper. Set aside. Divide the dough into 10 balls. Roll each ball into a "snake" about 10 inches long. Tie it into a knot (like the kind you make when tying your shoes) then wrap the ends around and through, tucking and pinching them into the knot. No matter how you shape your rolls, they will taste yummy. (**Tip**: *See the steps to making a knot in the pictorial.*)

5. While oven is preheating to 375°F, convection bake, transfer the knots to the lined baking sheet. Cover them with a slightly damp, clean dish towel so the dough can rise again or become "more puffy".

6. Paint the knots lightly with egg wash. Bake until golden brown. I begin checking for doneness at 14 minutes.

7. Remove from the oven and eat warm.

8. Store in an air-tight container to preserve softness.

MOTHER GOOSE MIX UP
Toss in golden raisins, Craisins, sultanas, chopped dates or dried figs for a flavorful and spirited twist.

CHAPTER 2

Dulces *and* Desserts

This chapter is dedicated to the **sweet** moments in our lives.

There's an expression in Chile, *endulza tu vida*, which means "sweeten your life." These recipes do just that. They aren't purposefully light or low-cal, but they are made from whole food ingredients and are full of love.

Take heart, dessert can be a part of a balanced diet. In our house, Axel and Rex selected Wednesday to be family dessert day. We choose and serve a dessert on Wednesdays. Everyone can eat dessert, whether we finish our peas (for example) or not. Giving sweets a place at the table lets the kids know that there is no shame in sugar. It's not for every day, but making space for all foods in your diet builds a healthy relationship with food based on inclusion and enjoyment, not restriction.

WHAT ARE LITTLE KIDS MADE OF?

WHAT ARE LITTLE BOYS MADE OF?

What are little boys made of?
Snips and snails
And puppy-dogs' tails,
That's what little boys are made of.

WHAT ARE LITTLE GIRLS MADE OF?

What are little girls made of?
Sugar and spice
And everything nice,
That's what little girls are made of.

CLASSIC CREAM CHEESE ICING

Makes:	4 cups	**Challenge Level:**	Piece of Cake
Contains:	Milk	**Active Time:**	15 minutes
Diet Type:	Gluten Free	**Total Time:**	20 minutes

This recipe makes a lot of icing. I like to keep Classic Cream Cheese Icing in the freezer and pull it out when I want to frost cakes, cookies, cinnamon rolls and other sweet treats. You can also make variations on this classic icing.

INGREDIENTS

- 1 cup (2 sticks) unsalted butter, softened
- 8 ounces (1 packet) cream cheese, softened
- 3⅓ cups powdered sugar
- 1 teaspoon vanilla extract

KIDS CAN

- Scrape down the sides of the bowl
- Sift the powdered sugar

WATCH OUT FOR

- Eating too much frosting!

INSTRUCTIONS

1. In a large mixing bowl, beat together butter and cream cheese until creamy and white, about 3 minutes. If you have a stand-up mixer, use the paddle attachment.
2. Scrape down the sides and bottom of the bowl to ensure all the butter and cream cheese have been incorporated.
3. Sift the powdered sugar using a hand sifter. (***Tip***: *If you don't have a sifter, set a mesh colander over a large bowl. Pour powdered sugar in the mesh colander and gently shake it over the bowl.*)
4. Add the vanilla extract and half of the powdered sugar. Beat some more then stop and add the rest of the powdered sugar. Continue beating until fluffy, creamy icing forms.
5. Taste. If it's not just right, add a bit more powdered sugar.
6. Store in the refrigerator or freeze in an airtight container for future use.

MOTHER GOOSE MIX UP

- For chocolate icing, add ¼ to ½ cup unsweetened cocoa powder
- For confetti icing, add ½ cup rainbow sprinkles

APPLE PIE

APPLE PIE

An apple pie, when it looks nice,
Would make one long to have a slice,
But if the taste should prove so, too,
I fear one slice would scarcely do.
So to prevent my asking twice,
Pray, Mama, cut a good large slice.

Making apple pie from scratch is just one of those things that gets easier
with time and practice...and patience. I guarantee the first attempt will be
tasty—like really, really, off the charts tasty—but it may not be pretty.
Keep at it. Baking pies does get easier and the results do get better, making
your time and effort totally worth it. Don't be surprised if, after some practice,
apple pie becomes your "signature dish." You know, the one food that
friends always ask you to bring to pot-luck dinners, end of year team
parties and school bake sales.

Turn to page 132 for a step-by-step pictorial on pie assembly!

Anytime you can make something in your own kitchen rather than buy it in a store, it will be fresher, purer and almost always healthier—even when it's dessert. Everything about this pie is fresh. There are no preservatives, additives or colorants. Whole food ingredients mixed together with love is what baking from scratch is all about.

MAMA'S APPLE PIE

Makes: One pie or 10 large slices
Contains: Milk, Egg, Wheat

Challenge Level: So Worth the Effort
Active Time: 1 hour 30 minutes
Total Time: 4 hours 30 minutes

INGREDIENTS

For the Filling:

- 2 teaspoons lemon juice
- 6 cups (about 5 large) red and green apples peeled and sliced thin
- 3 cups filtered water
- ½ cup brown sugar, packed
- ½ cup granulated sugar
- ⅓ cup cornstarch
- ½ teaspoon cinnamon
- 1 teaspoon McCormick Apple Cinnamon Naturally Flavored Sugar and Spice Blend
- Several shakes ground nutmeg
- 1 tablespoon unsalted butter

KIDS CAN

- Wash and dry the apples
- Squeeze the lemons
- Measure dry ingredients
- Sprinkle or shake seasonings
- Pinch, knead and roll the pastry
- Use cookie cutters to cut shapes from extra pastry for the top of the pie
- Paint pie with milk

WATCH OUT FOR

- Bubbling pots, hot oven and sharp objects

For the Pastry:

- 14 tablespoons unsalted butter straight-from-the-fridge-cold
- 2½ cups all-purpose flour
- 2 tablespoons granulated sugar
- 1 teaspoon salt
- 1 teaspoon McCormick Apple Cinnamon Naturally Flavored Sugar and Spice Blend

- 3 tablespoons milk plus more to paint the pastry before it goes into the oven
- Up to 2 tablespoons filtered water (only if your pastry isn't coming together)
- 1 to 2 tablespoons almond flour

INSTRUCTIONS ON NEXT PAGE

APPLE PIE FILLING

INSTRUCTIONS

For the Filling:

1. Drizzle lemon juice over the apple slices.
2. Place the water, sugars, cornstarch and spices in a skillet. Bring to a simmer, stir occasionally.
3. Bring the mixture to a boil and cook for 1 minute or until just thickened.
4. Add the apples to the pan and stir to coat with the sauce. Lower the heat to medium and cook until the apples have softened, 10 to 15 minutes.
5. Add the butter to the pan and stir until it has melted.
6. Cool the apple filling for 10 minutes, then transfer it to airtight containers and refrigerate or freeze until you're ready to use. If using the same day, allow filling to cool completely before putting it into pie crust (about 1 hour).

WHILE YOUR FILLING IS COOLING, MAKE THE APPLE PIE PASTRY!

For the Pastry:

7. Chop the butter in cubes and mix it in a bowl with the flour, sugar, salt and seasoning.
8. Use your fingers to cut in the butter (it's a pinching motion) with the dry ingredients until there are no chunks of butter left and your mix looks like bread-crumbs. You can also do this step in a food processor (***Tip:** Put all the dry ingredients in a food processor and pulse to mix. Add butter one cube at a time*)
9. Add milk and knead using your hands or add milk and mix in a food processor (***Tip:** Add milk while the food processor runs, 1 tablespoon at a time.*) Add water (if needed). After kneading or mixing the dough for 3 to 7 minutes the dough will begin to form a ball.
10. Divide the pastry crust in half and make 2 balls. Wrap each ball in plastic wrap and let them rest in the fridge for an hour. If you leave them in there longer (overnight, for example) let the pastry crust soften before rolling it.

MAMA'S APPLE PIE CONTINUED

KEEPING IT SIMPLE You don't have to paint the pie plate or pan with butter. This crust won't stick to the plate.

INSTRUCTIONS

To Assemble: (see step-by-step pictorial on next page)

11. Use a pastry mat and rolling pin to roll the first pastry ball into a circle. Save the other ball for later.

12. Roll from the center out and avoid rolling the pin off the edge of the pastry until the very end. Aim for a circle that is 4 inches larger than your pie plate.

13. Transition your pastry from the rolling pin to the pie plate being careful not to break it.

14. Lift the pastry so it falls into the pie plate to fit the corners, bottom, and sides. Press pastry into the side of the plate with your fingers to form a wall.

15. Roll your pin over the top of the pie plate to cut the pastry that is hanging over. Use a small knife to neaten up the edges.

16. Sprinkle the interior of the pie with almond flour. This will help absorb excess liquid from the pie filling and keep the bottom of your pie from going soggy.

17. Fill the pastry with apple filling.

18. Roll out the second pastry ball into a large circle, just 2 inches bigger than the pie plate. Gently transition your pastry from the rolling pin to the top of the pie.

19. Repeat step 15. Press around the inside of the top edge gently with your fingers to join the top and bottom.

20. Cut 3 or 4 slits in the top to vent steam.

21. Preheat oven to 350°F, convection bake.

22. Use pastry scraps to make decorations, like leaves, for the top of your pie. Paint top of pie with milk to "glue" the decorative leaves on top. (**Tip:** *If you do not decorate the top of your pie, you still need to paint it with milk.*)

23. Bake pie until golden, about 50 minutes.

24. Cool on a rack before serving. The pie keeps well, covered, at room temperature for 24 hours or refrigerated for up to 4 days. Serve warm with a scoop of vanilla ice cream.

MOTHER GOOSE MIX UP

Be a Pro at Rolling Dough: Cool pie dough rolls best. Dough that's too cold will crack when it's rolled; if too warm, it will stick to the rolling surface. Test your dough's firmness by pressing it with your fingers; they should leave a slight imprint.

HOW TO ASSEMBLE A PIE

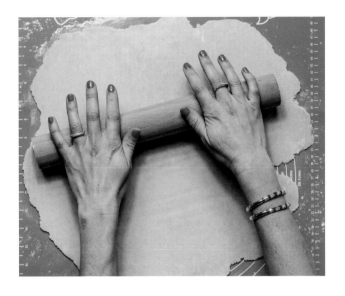

1. Use a pastry mat and rolling pin to roll the first pastry ball into a circle. Save the other ball for later.

2. Roll from the center out and avoid rolling the pin off the edge of the pastry until the very end. Aim for a circle that is 4 inches larger than your pie plate.

3. Transition your pastry from the rolling pin to the pie plate being careful not to break it.

   You don't have to paint the pie plate with butter. This crust won't stick to the plate.

4. Lift the pastry so it falls into the pie plate to fit the corners, bottom and sides. Press pastry into the side of the plate with your fingers to form a wall.

HOW TO ASSEMBLE A PIE

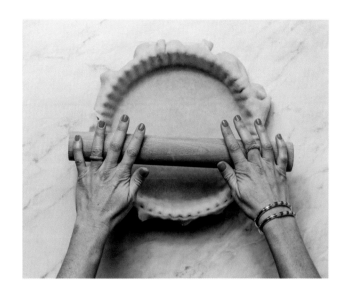

5. Roll your pin over the top of the pie plate to cut the pastry that is hanging over.

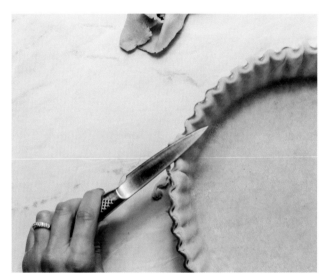

6. Use a small knife to neaten up the edges.

7. Sprinkle the interior of the pie with almond flour. This will help absorb excess liquid from the pie filling and keep the bottom of your pie from going soggy.

HOW TO ASSEMBLE A PIE

8. Fill the pastry with apple filling, or whatever pie filling you are using.

9. Roll out the second pastry ball into a large circle, just 2 inches bigger than the pie plate. Gently transition your pastry from the rolling pin to the top of the pie.

10. Repeat steps 5 and 6. Press around the inside of the top edge gently with your fingers to join the top and bottom.

HOW TO ASSEMBLE A PIE

11. Cut 3 or 4 slits in the top to vent steam.

12. Preheat oven to 350°F, convection bake.
    Paint pie with milk before putting it into the oven.

13. Use pastry scraps to make decorations, like leaves,
    for the top of your pie. Paint top of pie with milk
    to "glue" the decorative leaves on top.
    (**Tip:** *If you do not decorate the top of your pie,
    you still need to paint it with milk.*)

14. Bake pie until golden, about 50 minutes.

15. Cool on a rack before serving. The pie keeps well,
    covered, at room temperature for 24 hours, or
    refrigerated for up to 4 days. Serve warm with
    a scoop of vanilla ice cream.

THE KETTLE'S ON THE FIRE

The Kettle's On the Fire

The kettle's on the fire
And we'll all have tea
We'll also have a dumpling,
But nothing else there'll be.
A cup of tea that's piping hot,
Is just the thing to hit the spot.

TEA PARTY SWEETS

These recipes are inspired by the sweet side of tea time and they
are reminiscent of the soft, round, chewy deliciousness of a dumpling.

CHOCOLATE CAKE TRUFFLES

Makes: 18 Truffles
Contains: Milk, Egg, Wheat

Challenge Level: Just a Pinch Involved
Active Time: 45 minutes
Total Time: 1 hour 30 minutes

INGREDIENTS

- 1 cup granulated sugar
- ½ cup plus 6 tablespoons all-purpose flour
- Pinch of salt
- ¾ teaspoon baking powder
- ½ teaspoon baking soda
- 6 tablespoons cocoa powder
- 1 tablespoon vanilla extract

- ½ cup boiling filtered water
- ½ cup milk
- 1 egg
- ¼ cup plus 2 tablespoons canola oil
- Up to 1 cup **Classic Cream Cheese Icing** (p. 125)
- 1 cup melting chocolate (We like Ghiradelli Dark Chocolate Flavored Melting Wafers.)
- Sprinkles or other "pretties" for decoration

INSTRUCTIONS

1. Preheat the oven to 350°F.
2. Mix all dry ingredients in a large bowl – or in the bowl of your stand-up mixer using the whisk attachment.
3. Then add milk, egg, oil and vanilla. Beat at high speed for 2 minutes, lower power and add hot water.
4. Bake in a standard baking pan sprayed with cooking spray and lined with parchment paper for 25 to 30 minutes or until it passes the "Toothpick Test."
5. Allow cake to cool completely, then use your hands to crumble cake in a large bowl. Mix cake crumbles with the icing one spoonful at a time until you have a consistency that sticks together but won't stick to your hands.
6. Roll mixture into balls and refrigerate for 15 minutes.
7. While cake balls cool, put melting chocolate in a small, microwave-safe bowl and melt in the microwave in 30 second increments, stirring between each one. Be careful not to burn the chocolate. (**Tip:** *If most wafers are melted, usually stirring will melt any that remain.*)
8. Use a fork to lower and dip cold cake balls into the melted chocolate. Allow the excess chocolate to drip back into the bowl.
9. Place chocolate coated cake—now called a truffle—on a tray lined with parchment paper.
10. Immediately coat with decorative sprinkles or decorations of choice.
11. Refrigerate until ready to serve. Refrigerate leftover chocolate cake truffles in an airtight container.

Until I teamed up with my friend and self-taught Chef Silvana, I thought profiteroles were a "restaurant-only" dessert. The kind of perfect pastry that only professionals could get right. I was so wrong—profiteroles aren't hard to make at all. In fact, with Silvana to boost my confidence, I nailed our recipe on the first try! These profiteroles are filled with manjar, a type of dulce de leche that is 100% Chilean. Manjar is a sort of caramel that can be found in every grocery store and pastry shop in Chile. If you want to make your own (it's really easy), look to **Abuela's Dulce de Leche** recipe on page 143.

PROFITEROLES

Makes: 12 to 14 profiteroles
Contains: Milk, Egg, Wheat

Challenge Level: Just a Pinch Involved
Active Time: 30 minutes
Total Time: 1 hour

INGREDIENTS

- ½ cup filtered water
- 3½ tablespoons unsalted butter, room temperature
- ½ cup all-purpose flour
- 2 eggs, room temperature
- Manjar or **Abuela's Dulce de Leche** (p. 143) for filling

KIDS CAN

- Help you find the ingredients
- Pat down profiterole peaks with a wet finger

WATCH OUT FOR

- Distractions. You have to be on the ball when making the dough.

INSTRUCTIONS

For the Profiteroles:

1. In a medium pot, bring water and butter to boil.
2. Once water is boiling and butter has melted, pour in all the flour and whisk vigorously until a film forms in the bottom of the pot, the dough pulls apart and begins to form a ball.
   Remove the pot from heat and let it cool for 5 minutes.
3. Add eggs one at a time with a wooden spoon, beating well into the mixture each time.
   You are creating a dough that resembles a thick paste.
4. Preheat the oven to 400°F.
5. Pour or spoon the paste into a piping bag fitted with a round tip and pipe "blobs" the size of a ping pong ball onto a baking sheet lined with parchment paper.
6. With your wet index finger pat down peaks that may have formed.
   (**Tip**: A wet finger prevents profiterole paste from sticking to your hand).
7. Bake for 15 minutes, then lower heat to 350°F and bake for an additional 15 minutes.
   Don't open oven until the second bake is complete.
8. Allow to cool, then fill with manjar or dulce de leche, which you also pipe in with the piping bag (see below).
9. Sprinkle with confectioners sugar or drizzle with caramel or chocolate sauce.

To Fill:

10. Use a piping bag fitted with a round tip and fill it with dulce de leche or your filling of preference (if filling with ice cream, see step 12 below).
11. With that same tip, poke a hole in the bottom of the profiterole and squeeze the filling in.
12. If filling profiteroles with ice cream, cut the profiterole in half, fill with a scoop of ice cream and re-assemble the profiterole like you are making a profiterole sandwich. Drizzle with chocolate sauce or caramel.

NUTRITION NIBBLE Parents often use dessert as a bribe. When it comes to dessert, try saying: "When everyone is finished eating, we will have dessert." This ensures dessert isn't associated with rewards. Instead, dessert is a 'given' on those days that you (Mom and Dad) decide to serve it. It's just another part of the meal instead of something you earn.

ABUELA'S (GRANNY'S) DULCE DE LECHE

Makes: 1½ cups
Contains: Milk
Diet Type: Gluten Free Option

Challenge Level: Piece of Cake
Active Time: 15 minutes
Total Time: 2 hours 15 minutes

INGREDIENTS

- (1) 14-ounce can sweetened condensed milk (We like Borden Eagle Brand Sweetened Condensed Milk, which is gluten free)
- Filtered water

INSTRUCTIONS

1. Peel the label off the can of condensed milk and throw it away.
2. Fill a large deep pot with water. Place the can of condensed milk inside.
3. Bring water to a boil.
4. Maintain the boil for 2 hours. Top up the pot with additional water so the can remains covered in water. (**Tip**: *This is a good opportunity to talk about science in the kitchen. Water at very cold temperatures becomes solid ice, then it is liquid and at boiling temperatures becomes steam*).
5. Use tongs or a ladle to remove can from pot. Allow the can to cool completely.
6. Recite some magic words like "*Abracadabra*" while you and your child open the can together. Reveal the results—the condensed milk has caramelized into perfect, creamy, dulce de leche as if by magic.

KIDS CAN

- Set the timer
- Watch as you reveal the manjar after cooking
- Learn the Spanish word for Grandma (Abuela)

WATCH OUT FOR

- Forgetting to top up the pot with water while can boils
- Removing the can of condensed milk when it is hot

MOTHER GOOSE MIX UP   Use cold dulce de leche as a dip for fruit or warm it and drizzle over ice cream.

BAT, BAT COME UNDER MY CAP

BAT, BAT COME UNDER MY CAP

Bat, bat, come under my cap
And I'll give you a slice of bacon;
And when I bake,
I'll give you a cake,
If I am not mistaken.

NUTRITION NIBBLE Including dessert as part of your family routine has benefits you might not expect. When dessert is 'a given' instead of something a child earns, they don't gorge themselves on it. Instead, they eat as much as they are hungry for, knowing that they will get dessert again.

MAPLE BACON CAKE  MAPLE ICING

Makes:	1 cake or 16 slices	**Challenge Level:**	So Worth the Effort
Contains:	Milk, Egg, Wheat, Tree Nuts	**Active Time:**	1 hour
		Total Time:	4 hours (includes 2 hours of cooling time)

Are you achin' for some bacon? While we don't make bacon or cake very often, when we do, we go "whole hog." The combination of maple and bacon and cake is positively, surprisingly scrumptious. It's sweet and salty combination that makes grown ups and kids alike smile with appreciation... And go back for another bite!

INGREDIENTS

- 2¼ cups all-purpose flour
  (**Tip**: *Instead of buying cake flour, you can mix cornstarch and all-purpose flour to get that fluffy and soft texture cakes are famous for*)
- ¼ cup cornstarch
- 1 cup brown sugar, packed
- ½ teaspoon salt
- ⅔ cup (11 tablespoons) cold, unsalted butter
- 2 teaspoons baking powder
- ½ teaspoon baking soda
- ½ teaspoon ground cinnamon
- 1½ teaspoons McCormick Vanilla Cinnamon Sugar and Spice Blend divided
  ¼ teaspoon ground nutmeg
- 2 eggs
- 1½ cups buttermilk (**Tip**: *You can make your own buttermilk, see instructions below.*)
- ½ cup maple syrup plus 2 tablespoons, divided
- 5 low sodium bacon strips, cooked crispy and crumbled
- ½ cup chopped walnuts
- 3 cups **Classic Cream Cheese Icing** (p. 125), divided

KIDS CAN

- Measure dry ingredients
- Crack eggs with help
- Prepare cake pans with cooking spray and parchment paper

WATCH OUT FOR

- Hot oven
- Cakes that are too warm or icing that is too cold make decorating impossible

INSTRUCTIONS ON NEXT PAGE

INSTRUCTIONS

For the Cake:

1. Preheat oven to 350° F, convection bake.

2. To make the buttermilk, combine 1½ cups milk with 1 teaspoon (or a good squirt) fresh lemon juice. Stir buttermilk and set aside.

3. In a large bowl combine flour, cornstarch, brown sugar and salt.

4. Cut in butter until crumbly.

5. Combine the baking powder, baking soda, salt, nutmeg and 1 teaspoon of McCormick Vanilla Cinnamon Sugar and Spice Blend.

6. In a separate bowl, whisk the eggs, buttermilk, ½ cup of the maple syrup until well blended. Gradually stir into flour mixture until combined.

7. Pour batter into three 4-inch round baking pans sprayed with cooking spray and lined on the bottom with parchment paper.

8. Bake 20 to 25 minutes or until each cake passes the "Toothpick Test." (**Tip**: *Not all ovens heat evenly, so sometimes one cake pan is ready before the others. Be sure each pan passes the "Toothpick Test" before removing from the oven*).

9. Cool on a wire rack. Allow to cool completely before decorating - about 2 hours in the fridge.

MAPLE BACON CAKE *AND* MAPLE ICING

INSTRUCTIONS

For the Maple Icing:

10. Start with **Classic Cream Cheese Icing** (p. 125)

11. Add 2 tablespoons maple syrup and remaining ½ teaspoon of Vanilla Cinnamon Sugar and Spice Blend. Whip icing until the flavors are incorporated, about 2 minutes.

12. Taste the frosting. Adjust spices, if necessary.

Assemble and Decorate the Cake:

13. Set cakes on the counter. Using a sharp bread knife, cut off the dome so you have 3 flat topped cakes. *(**Tip:** Bend down so you are eye level with the top of the cake in order to cut level horizontally.)*

14. Place a cake board on top of your turntable. *(**Tip:** A Lazy Susan or cake turntable and a bench scraper make decorating easy-peasy!)* Measure out 1 cup of the Maple Cream Cheese Icing for the crumb coat.

15. Take a big spoon of crumb coat icing and place it in the middle of the turntable. This will act like "glue" to hold down the cake.

16. Place the first cake layer on top of the icing.

17. Smear icing on top of the first layer of cake. Don't worry if it goes over the sides, you will scrape all the excess icing away later. Continue until you have all three layers iced.

18. Take a bench scraper and smooth all the overflow icing onto the sides of the cake— this crumb coat captures cake crumbs so they don't show up in the outer, decorative icing layers.

19. If your icing is melting, put cake in the fridge for 10 minutes. Decorate the outside with the remaining icing, crumbled bacon and walnuts.

CURLY LOCKS

CURLY LOCKS

Curly Locks, Curly Locks,
Will you be mine?
You shall not wash dishes,
Nor feed the swine,
But sit on a cushion
And sew a fine seam,
And sup upon strawberries,
Sugar and cream.

STRAWBERRIES ~AND~ CREAM ICE CAKE

Makes: (4) 4-inch cakes or 16 slices

Contains: Milk, Wheat

(potentially contains egg in waffle cone)

Challenge Level: So Worth the Effort

Active Time: 1 hour

Total Time: 5 hours (includes 4 hours freeze time)

INGREDIENTS

For the Waffle Cone Crust:

- 24 store-bought waffle ice cream cones
- 3 tablespoons brown sugar
- 6 tablespoons unsalted butter, melted
- 1 tablespoon McCormick Birthday Cake Naturally Flavored Sugar and Spice Blend
- Liberal shakes of cinnamon

For the Strawberries and Cream Filling:

- 3 cups whole fresh strawberries
- 1 cup granulated sugar, divided
- ¼ cup sour cream
- 1 tablespoon McCormick Birthday Cake Naturally Flavored Sugar and Spice Blend
- ½ teaspoon vanilla extract
- 3 cups whipping cream
- A few handfuls of strawberries hulled and sliced to decorate the top

KIDS CAN

- Wash strawberries and pat dry
- Lay strawberries and sugar to rest in a bowl
- Break the waffle cones
- Trace and cut the parchment paper with guidance
- Spray the spring form pan with cooking spray
- Pat down the crust
- Set the timer
- Mash strawberries and sour cream
- Decorate

WATCH OUT FOR

- Strawberry thieves

INSTRUCTIONS ON NEXT PAGE

INSTRUCTIONS

For the Strawberries:

1. Wash strawberries and pat dry.
2. Hull strawberries and cut into chunks.
3. Rest in a large covered bowl mixed with ¾ cup granulated sugar.
4. Make the crust and whip the cream.

For the Crust:

5. Preheat the oven to 350°F.
6. Use your fingers to break apart waffle cones then put into your food processor and pulse until fine (a few chunks are OK).
7. Place butter and brown sugar in a microwave-safe bowl. Heat until melted. Stir to incorporate. Add the cinnamon and McCormick Birthday Cake Blend. Stir to incorporate.

NUTRITION NIBBLE Strawberries belong to the "dirty dozen," a group of produce that have the most pesticide residue as measured by the United States Pesticide Data Program. As of 2019, the Environmental Working Group reports that one-third of all non-organic strawberries contain ten or more pesticide residues. So, for strawberries and the remaining 11 crops in this list, try to buy organic and never eat these (or any produce, really) without rinsing with water first.

STRAWBERRIES AND CREAM ICE CAKE

INSTRUCTIONS

For the Crust (continued):

8. Add sweetened butter to the food processor. Pulse until you get a consistency that resembles thick, moist sand.

9. Prepare (4) 4-inch round spring form pans (can substitute an 11-inch round spring form pan to make one massive ice cake). Spray bottom and sides with cooking spray and fit a circle of parchment paper to the bottom.

10. Scoop waffle cone crust into the pan and pat down with your hands until even.

11. Pack the crust even tighter with an inverted straight-sided drinking glass. Pack and press the crust to fill the entire bottom of the pan, making sure to get the crust all the way to the edges. Crust should be about ⅛ to ¼ inch thick.

12. Bake crust for about 10 minutes or until golden and fragrant.

13. Set aside or set in the refrigerator to cool.

For the Strawberries and Cream Filling:

14. In a large, cold bowl combine whipping cream with vanilla and remaining ¼ cup granulated sugar.

15. Whip cream until it doubles or almost triples in volume. *(**Tip:** I use a stand-up mixer with the whisk attachment).*

16. Set 1 cup whipped cream aside to top the ice cake. Cover it with plastic wrap and refrigerate until ready to decorate.

17. Go back to the resting strawberries and add sour cream and McCormick Birthday Cake Blend.

18. Mix and mash the contents of the strawberry bowl together with the back of a fork.

19. Fold mashed strawberries into whipped cream. *(**Tip:** A rubber spatula works well for this.)*

Assemble the Ice Cake:

20. Check that the waffle cone crust is completely cool. If it is, spoon in whipped strawberries and cream. Stop ½ inch before the top of the pan.

21. Cover with plastic wrap and put in the freezer for 4 hours or overnight.

22. Before serving, open each spring form pan and remove the sides. Decorate each ice cake with ¼ cup reserved whipped cream and sliced strawberries as desired.

23. Run a knife under hot water, then cut the cake.

THE DIRTY DOZEN

1. Strawberries	5. Grapes	9. Tomatoes
2. Spinach	6. Peaches	10. Celery
3. Nectarines	7. Cherries	11. Potatoes
4. Apples	8. Pears	12. Sweet Bell Peppers

PAT-A-CAKE

PAT-A-CAKE

Pat-a-cake, pat-a-cake, baker's man,
Bake me a cake as fast as you can.
Roll it and pat it and mark it with a "B"
And put it in the oven for Baby and me!

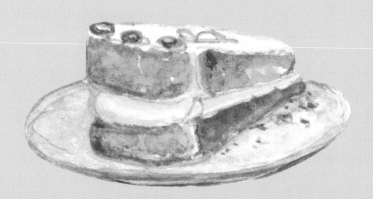

Pat-a-cake is the first nursery rhyme my boys learned by heart and a
great one for your littles because you can make it into a partner game.
Sit cross legged across from each other and clap hands together to the tune.
Then roll your hands and pat your knees. Expect lots of laughter and squeals
when you reach out to draw a "B" on their tummies. When you make this
recipe together, make sure to clap, roll, pat and of course, taste!

NUTRITION NIBBLE This birthday biscotti is a festive alternative to traditional birthday cake. You can serve it at the party in place of cake or put a biscotti cookie inside each child's party bag to take home as a favor—so much better than a bunch of candy. Using the **Blow Wind Blow Gluten-Free Flour Blend** (p. 219) makes a firm biscotti that isn't rock hard, perfect for tiny teeth.

Twice-Baked Birthday Biscotti

Makes: 30 biscotti cookies

Contains: Egg, Tree Nuts

Diet Type: Gluten Free, Dairy Free

Challenge Level: Piece of Cake

Active Time: 30 minutes

Total Time: 2 hours

INGREDIENTS

- 3½ to 4 cups **Blow Wind Blow Gluten-Free Flour Blend** (p. 219) or store-bought
- 1 teaspoon baking powder
- ½ teaspoon salt
- 1 cup vegetable oil
- 1¼ cups granulated sugar, divided
- 3 eggs
- 1 tablespoon almond extract
- ⅔ cup rainbow sprinkles

KIDS CAN

- Sift the dry ingredients
- Roll the dough
- Dump in the sprinkles
- Pat in the decorative sugar
- Sing

WATCH OUT FOR

- Forgetting to bake the biscotti twice
- Sharp knives
- Hot oven

INSTRUCTIONS

1. Preheat the oven to 350°F, convection bake.
2. Use a flour mill or a fine mesh colander to sift together flour, baking powder and salt in a medium bowl.
3. In a separate bowl or with your stand-up mixer, whisk together oil and 1 cup of granulated sugar. Add eggs, one at a time and whisk until well-blended. Add almond extract.
4. Pour flour mixture into sugar mixture and stir until just combined. If dough is sticky, add up to ½ cup more flour.
5. Dump in rainbow sprinkles and stir (**Tip**: *Waiting to stir in sprinkles after you have created the dough keeps the colors from bleeding).*
6. Divide dough in half. Roll each half into a 9 x 4-inch rectangle or slab.
7. Set "slabs" about a hand's width apart on a large baking sheet lined with parchment paper or a Silpat.
8. Sprinkle tops with ¼ cup granulated sugar. Use your fingertips to gently pat sugar into the dough.
9. Bake for 25 minutes. Remove from the oven and reduce the temperature to 300°F.
10. Cool first-baked cookie slabs for 15 minutes, then transfer to a wire rack.
11. Once completely cool, use a serrated knife to cut cookies on a slight diagonal into (24) 1-inch thick biscotti.
12. Place biscotti, cut side down, back on the parchment-lined baking sheet.
13. Bake a second time, until biscotti are lightly golden on both sides, about 15 more minutes.
14. Leave biscotti on their baking sheet and set on a wire rack to cool completely before serving.

NUTRITION NIBBLE A balanced diet makes room for dessert. Restricting food (like sugar and treats) can backfire on parents. Kids need to learn how to incorporate sweets into their diet from you. Allowing these foods at home lets children know they don't need to sneak these desserts—they can be enjoyed in moderation as a family.

BEST EVER COCONUT CAKE

Makes: 1 cake or 16 slices
Contains: Milk, Egg, Wheat

Challenge Level: So Worth the Effort
Active Time: 1 hour
Total Time: 4 hours

INGREDIENTS

For the Cake:

- 1 stick unsalted butter
- 3 tablespoons coconut oil
- ¾ cups granulated sugar
- 1½ tablespoons vanilla extract
- 3 eggs, room temperature
- 1¾ cups all-purpose flour
- 3 teaspoons baking powder
- ½ cup plain full-fat yogurt
- ¼ cup milk
- ½ teaspoon salt
- **Classic Cream Cheese Icing** (p. 125)

KIDS CAN

- Crack eggs with help
- Sift dry ingredients
- Prepare cake pans with cooking spray and parchment paper
- Wash berries and pat dry

WATCH OUT FOR

- Hot oven
- Cakes that are too warm or icing that is too cold make decorating impossible

INSTRUCTIONS ON NEXT PAGE

IF YOU THINK YOU HATE
COCONUT – THINK AGAIN!
YOU WILL LOVE THIS CAKE!

INSTRUCTIONS

For the Cake:

1. Preheat oven to 350°F, convection bake.
2. Cream butter, coconut oil and granulated sugar in your stand-up mixer using the whisk attachment.
3. Add eggs, one at a time, to the creamed butter and sugar. (**Tip:** *Give children a little bowl to crack their eggs into to avoid any shell pieces getting into the cake batter.*)
4. In a separate bowl, combine flour, baking powder and salt, then sift to remove any lumps. This improves the texture.
5. If using a stand-up mixer, change to paddle attachment and add sifted ingredients a little at a time until batter is smooth.
6. Pour batter into three or four 4-inch round baking pans coated with cooking spray and lined on the bottom with parchment paper. Stop filling at the half-way mark to avoid a big mess in your oven. (**Note:** To make a two-tier cake like in the picture, use two different size cake pans and make a double batch of cake and icing. I find it is harder to frost a two-tier cake, so if this is your "first rodeo," maybe start with the one-tier cake.)
7. Bake 20 to 25 minutes or until each cake passes the "Toothpick Test." (**Tip:** *Not all ovens heat evenly, so sometimes one cake pan is ready before the others. Be sure each pan passes the "Toothpick Test" before removing from the oven.*)
8. Cool cakes on a wire rack, then transfer to refrigerator. Allow to cool completely before decorating, about 2 hours.

BEST EVER COCONUT CAKE

CONTINUED

INSTRUCTIONS

Assemble and Decorate the Cake:

9. Set cakes on the counter. Using a sharp bread knife, cut off the dome so you have 3 (or 4) flat-topped cakes. *(**Tip:** Bend down so you are eye level with the top of the cake in order to cut level horizontally.)*

10. Place a cake board on top of your turntable. *(**Tip:** A Lazy Susan or cake turntable and a bench scraper make decorating easy-peasy!)*

11. Measure out 1½ cups of the **Classic Cream Cheese Frosting** for the crumb coat. Leave the rest of the icing out so it's at room temperature for the final coat.

12. Take a big spoon of crumb coat icing and place it in the middle of the cake board. This will act like "glue" to hold down the cake.

13. Place the first cake layer on top of the icing.

14. Smear icing on top of the first layer of cake. Don't worry if it goes over the sides, you will scrape all the excess icing away later. Continue until you have all layers stacked, then smear any remaining icing on the sides.

15. Take a bench scraper and smooth all the overflow icing from the top of the cake onto the sides—this crumb coat captures cake crumbs so they don't show up in the outer, decorative icing layers. *(**Tip:** Set this "crumby" icing aside. You can mix it with the cake you trimmed when leveling the layers to make a cake truffle mix up. See recipe page 139.)*

16. Put cake in the fridge for 10 minutes.

17. Decorate the outside with the remaining icing, blueberries and blackberries.

MOTHER GOOSE MIX UP

I've written this as a cake recipe, but it works just as well for cupcakes. Just reduce cooking time and simplify your decoration game.

A PILLOW SHAKEN

A PILLOW SHAKEN

A pillow shaken in the sky,
See how all the feathers fly,
Little snowflakes soft and light
Make the trees and meadows white.

Smooth, white and lightweight, it's a fun surprise when you find chocolate
chips inside these cookies. My mom used to make these with her grandmother.
My Great Grandma Lacey would shave bars of chocolate and whisk the meringue
by hand (quite a workout) when she baked with my mom. Two generations later,
her 21st century counterpart (that's me) is just a bit less inclined to make baking
a workout. I use chocolate chips and a stand-up mixer. Progress or perfection?
Who cares! These pillow cookies have passed the taste-tests of time.

CHOCOLATE CHIP MERINGUE COOKIES

Makes: 18 cookies

Contains: Milk, Egg

Diet Type: Gluten Free

Challenge Level: Piece of Cake

Active Time: 30 minutes

Total Time: 2 hours

INGREDIENTS

- 2 egg whites, room temperature
- ½ teaspoon cream of tartar
- ⅛ teaspoon salt
- ¾ cup granulated sugar
- ¼ teaspoon vanilla extract
- ¾ cup semisweet chocolate chips

KIDS CAN

- Crack eggs with help
- Prepare baking sheet
- Make **Tempera Paint** with the yolks (p. 231)

WATCH OUT FOR

- Hot oven
- Missing chocolate chips (you'll want extra chocolate chips around for your little cookie helpers)

INSTRUCTIONS

1. Combine the egg whites, salt, vanilla and cream of tartar in a bowl. Beat with a stand-up mixer using the whisk attachment. Beat until frothy, soft peaks form.
2. Add the sugar very gradually, beating all the while. Continue beating until the meringue is glossy and stiff, with a shaving cream-like consistency. This step takes me 6 or 7 minutes.
3. Fold in chocolate chips.
4. Line a baking sheet with parchment paper.
   Preheat the oven to 320°F and place the oven rack in the middle position.
5. Drop heaping mounds of meringue onto the lined baking sheet. I use 2 spoons—one to scoop and one to scrape the meringue onto the baking sheet. Allow 2 fingers-width distance between each one.
6. Bake for 30 minutes, then turn off the oven and let the cookies sit in the oven for 30 more minutes.
7. Remove meringue pillows from the oven and let them cool completely so the chocolate chips can firm up before removing the cookies from the parchment paper.
8. The cookies are crisp on the outside and gooey on the inside and incredibly light, fluffy and fragile.
9. If you don't eat them all, store leftovers in a resealable plastic bag or airtight container for several days.
   (***Tip***: *Climate may affect your cookies. In a dry climate, you shouldn't have any problems with soft or gooey meringue cookies. But things can go wrong if you live in a more humid area. If you do run into problems with soft or sticky meringues, try baking them just a bit longer.*)

CHERRY ON TOP

CAN YOU GUESS THE ANSWER
TO THIS RIDDLE?

As I went through the garden gap
Who should I meet but Dick Redcap!
A stick in his hand, a stone in his throat:
If you'll tell me this riddle
I'll give you a groat.

Answer: Cherry

There are as many ways to customize a thumbprint cookie as there are individual thumbprints. The Cherry on Top Thumbprint Cookie is the biscuit of my childhood. Gran and I would take half a day to create several batches of thumbprint cookies, which we filled with cherry pie filling. My version uses cherry jam, which is bright, happy and makes it easier for littles to "put a cherry on top."

P.S. A groat is a type of silver coin used long ago.
It was worth about as much as a US nickel (five cents).

TIP:
Children use their thumb, but for adults, the index finger makes a better sized imprint.

CHERRY ON TOP THUMBPRINT COOKIES

Makes: 30 cookies

Contains: Milk, Egg, Wheat, Tree Nuts

Challenge Level: Just a Pinch Involved

Active Time: 1 hour

Total Time: 1 hour 30 minutes (includes chilling time)

INGREDIENTS

- ⅔ cup unsalted butter
- ½ cup granulated sugar
- 2 eggs, whites and yolks separated
- 1 teaspoon vanilla extract
- 1 teaspoon almond extract
- 1½ cups all-purpose flour
- 1 cup sliced blanched almonds, chopped fine
- 1 jar cherry jam

KIDS CAN

- Paint dough with egg white
- Dent the dough with fingers
- Set the timer

WATCH OUT FOR

- Don't eat raw cookie dough (no matter how tempting)
- Hot oven
- Over baking

INSTRUCTIONS

1. In a stand-up mixer with the paddle attachment or with an electric mixer, cream butter and sugar together.
2. Add the egg yolks, vanilla and almond extracts. Continue to cream.
3. Beat in flour to make a soft dough.
4. Wrap the dough in plastic wrap and chill for 30 minutes.
5. Preheat the oven to 375°F. Spray a baking sheet with cooking spray.
6. Grease a teaspoon and scoop dough into teaspoon sized balls.
7. Whip egg whites.
8. Use a silicone brush to paint each cookie dough ball with the whipped egg white. Immediately roll in almonds.
9. Place almond coated cookie dough on the prepared baking sheet. Continue until all the cookie dough is used, placing cookies two-fingers width apart.
10. Press a dent in the center of each cookie with your thumb or index finger.
11. Bake 10 to 12 minutes or until golden brown on the bottom and no longer doughy in the center.
12. Fit cherry jam in the dent you made with your thumb. (**Tip:** *Do this as soon as the cookies come out of the oven to help "set" the cherry on top.*)
13. Cool on a wire rack and serve with **Classic Agua de Piña** (p. 195).

LITTLE MISS MUFFET

LITTLE MISS MUFFET

Little Miss Muffet
Sat on a tuffet,
Eating her curds and whey;
Along came a spider,
Who sat down beside her
And frightened Miss Muffet away.

For a fun spin on curds and whey, I dreamed up this combination of
paper-thin pancakes and creamy lemon curd. You may have seen whey
on your supplement aisle as an isolated protein powder. But before whey
becomes a supplement, which most kids don't need, it is the high-quality
protein found in milk. Serve crepes and lemon curd with a glass of milk and
I wager not even a spider could scare you away from this tasty treat.

NUTRITION NIBBLE

A crepe sounds fancy, but in essence, it is just a really, really, *really* thin pancake.
You can serve crepes flat, folded or rolled. Mixing up the look reduces picky eating
(this is an example of serving a familiar food like pancakes in an unfamiliar way...folded!)

POPPY SEED CREPES ⟨WITH⟩ LEMON CURD

Makes: 10 crepes

Contains: Milk, Egg, Wheat

Challenge Level: Piece of Cake

Active Time: 30 minutes

Total Time: 30 minutes (cooking 1 crepe at a time)

INGREDIENTS

- 1 cup all-purpose flour
- ¾ to 1 cup cold filtered water
- 1 egg
- ½ tablespoon unsalted butter, melted
- Pinch of salt
- Pinch of granulated sugar
  (if you like your crepes a little sweet)
- Sprinkle of poppy seeds, as many as you like
- Zest of ½ a lemon
  or ½ teaspoon lemon extract
- Vegetable oil, enough to barely coat the
  bottom of your frying pan

KIDS CAN

- Whisk the batter
- Shake in the poppy seeds

WATCH OUT FOR

- Hot frying pan

INSTRUCTIONS

1. Mix all of the ingredients together in a bowl and whisk to remove lumps.
2. Warm a nonstick frying pan to medium temperature, add just a drizzle of vegetable oil. With a soup spoon, add the batter to the pan. Gently swirl the pan until the bottom is covered with a thin layer of batter.
3. Wait until the entire crepe is dry on top, about 3 minutes, then flip.
4. The crepe is ready when it has a golden color on both sides.
5. Serve each crepe with 2 tablespoons **Lemon Curd** recipe on the next page.

LEMON CURD CAN BE MADE
UP TO 1 WEEK IN ADVANCE.

COVER IT WITH PLASTIC WRAP
SO A WEIRD SKIN DOESN'T
FORM ON TOP.

NUTRITION NIBBLE

Lemons have a tart taste and a pleasant smell that seems to enhance the flavor of many foods and drinks. They are also high in vitamin C and soluble fiber.

LEMON CURD

Makes: About 1½ cups
Contains: Milk, Egg
Diet Type: Gluten Free

Challenge Level: Just a Pinch Involved (requires active whisking)
Active Time: 20 minutes
Total Time: 30 minutes

INGREDIENTS

- 3 eggs
- 1 cup granulated sugar
- ½ cup fresh lemon juice
- 4 tablespoons unsalted butter, cubed
- 1 tablespoon lemon zest (optional)

KIDS CAN

- Scrub the lemons
- Roll the lemons
- Juice the lemons

WATCH OUT FOR

- Any tiny cuts on fingers or hands will burn if lemon juice gets inside
- Hot stove

INSTRUCTIONS

1. Set lemon on the table and roll with the palm of your hand. This will loosen up the juices inside.
2. Squeeze the lemon juice into a bowl.
3. In a small saucepan over medium heat, whisk eggs, sugar and lemon juice until blended.
4. Add butter and stir until incorporated.
5. Cook, whisking constantly, until mixture thickens, about 10 minutes.
   You'll know curd is ready when it passes the "Spoon Test." (**Tip**: *Curd continues to thicken as it cools.*)
6. No matter how well you whisk, some little bits of egg will make the curd lumpy.
   For a silky, smooth texture, pass the warm curd through a fine mesh strainer before transferring to a jar to cool.
7. Stir in lemon zest (if using)
8. Once cool, cover and place in the refrigerator until you're ready to use.
9. Use to fill **Poppy Seed Crepes**, or use as a variation for **Thumbprint Cookies** on page 171.

MOTHER GOOSE MIX UP Don't limit yourself to lemons! You can make curd from other citrus fruits like limes, oranges or grapefruit.

CURDY, CURDY CUSTARD

CURDY, CURDY CUSTARD

Curdy, curdy custard, green snot pie,

All mixed up with a dead dog's eye,

Slap it on a butty, nice and thick,

And drink it down with a cold cup of sick.

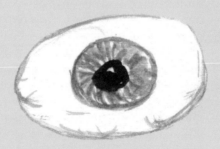

Here is one of those icky nursery rhymes that I would like to skip, but the boys love it. Let's face it—kids can be gross and it is the very grossness of this verse that makes it irresistible to them. When dreaming up something that would be reminiscent of curdy custard, but still a dish you'd like to eat, tapioca sprung to mind. It's slippery (yet satisfying), smooth and sweet.

It was Axel and Rex's idea to add grapes for eyeballs—though it grossed me out a bit, I obliged.

NUTRITION NIBBLE

Tapioca is gluten free, nut free and grain free, so it won't cause problems for family members with celiac disease, gluten sensitivity or nut allergies. A high-carbohydrate, high-calorie food, it is an excellent choice for kids who need to gain weight. Load up on the tasty toppings in this recipe: grapes and hazelnuts, which are rich in polyphenols, the active natural compounds that promote health in a range of areas, including brain, heart and gut function.

*Make sure to try our **Mote con Huesillos** drink on page 207.*

HAZELNUT TAPIOCA CUSTARD

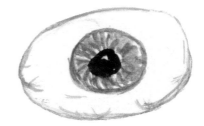

Makes: 3 cups

Contains: Milk, Egg, Tree Nuts

Diet Type: Gluten Free

Challenge Level: Piece of Cake

Active Time: 1 hour

Total Time: 1 hour 15 minutes (plus overnight soaking)

INGREDIENTS

- ½ cup small pearl tapioca (do not use instant)
- 2½ to 3 cups whole milk
- ¼ teaspoon salt
- 2 eggs, room temperature
- ¼ cup brown sugar
- ¼ cup granulated sugar
- 1 teaspoon vanilla extract
- Green grapes, sliced
- Hazelnuts, chopped (for garnish)

KIDS CAN

- Rinse tapioca in a colander
- Measure dry ingredients
- Stir in grapes and crushed hazelnuts

WATCH OUT FOR

- Grapes and nuts can be a choking hazard. Be sure to cut into smaller pieces for children under two years.

INSTRUCTIONS

1. Look at your tapioca package instructions. Soak if required.
2. Remove eggs from the refrigerator and allow them to come to room temperature. Make them a bath of warm (not hot) water to speed this process up.
3. Pass the tapioca through a fine mesh colander. Measure the milk and add salt. In a large, deep saucepan, set to medium-high heat, combine tapioca and salted milk. Bring to a simmer, stirring occasionally. Then reduce heat to the lowest setting and gently cook tapioca for about 30 minutes (depending on your tapioca brand it may be less or more).
4. Meanwhile, in a small bowl, beat eggs with an electric mixer until fluffy. Take ¼ cup of hot tapioca from the pot and slowly whisk it into the egg mixture. This process equalizes the temperature of the eggs to the cooking tapioca.
5. Pour the egg mixture into the pot, stir to combine. Continue to cook on low heat until a pudding forms, about 10 minutes. Do not let the pudding boil or the custard will curdle (and **that** really **is** gross).
6. Stir in vanilla. Allow to cool 15 minutes before serving.
7. Stir in cut green grapes. Serve warm or chilled with a sprinkle of crushed hazelnuts and more grapes on top.

Upstairs, downstairs

Upstairs, downstairs

Upstairs, downstairs, upon my lady's window,
There I saw a cup of sack and a race of ginger,
Apples at the fire and nuts to crack,
And a little boy in the cream pot up to his neck.

Many families leave cookies for Santa Claus at Christmas, but our family
makes these Spiced Baked Apples for Santa to share with his reindeer.

Like most herbs and spices, ginger has a slew of health benefits and is virtually calorie free. Ginger can aid digestion and relieve nausea. Fresh ginger can be spicy or mild depending on its age, so a little bit can go a long way.

SPICED APPLE CREAM POT

Makes: 4 filled apples

Contains: Tree Nuts

Diet Type: Gluten Free, Dairy Free

Challenge Level: Just a Pinch Involved

Active Time: 45 minutes

Total Time: 1 hour

INGREDIENTS

- 4 small red apples
- 4 teaspoons honey, divided
- ¼ cup extra virgin olive oil, divided
- 1 cup almond milk
- 1 finger (or a 3 inch piece) of fresh ginger
- 1½ tablespoons cornstarch
- 1 tablespoon maple syrup
- 1 handful pistachios, plus extra for garnish
- 1 handful almonds
- ⅛ cup dried apricot, roughly chopped
- 3 tablespoons apple cider
- Pinch of salt

KIDS CAN

- Wash apples and pat dry
- Paint apples with honey and olive oil
- Squeeze filling into baked apples
- Drizzle filled apple pots with cream glaze

WATCH OUT FOR

- Coring apples takes practice, it's easy to go too far
- Sharp blades of food processor
- Hot oven

INSTRUCTIONS

1. Wash apples and pat dry. Preheat the oven to 375°F.
2. Cut off the top of each apple. Carefully core each apple, leave it whole and make sure that the cavity is around 1 inch in diameter. (**Tip**: After you core the apple, you may have to scoop out a little more with a small spoon.)
3. In a small bowl, stir together 2 teaspoons each of olive oil and honey.
4. Set cored apples in a baking dish. Brush apples with oil-honey mixture and bake for 20 minutes, then set aside.
5. Peel and grate ginger. Place it in a bowl with almond milk, cornstarch and maple syrup. Stir to combine.
6. Cook in the microwave for 4 minutes, stopping to whisk every 30 seconds. The sauce starts to thicken about 3 minutes into the process. When sauce passes the "Spoon Test", cover with plastic wrap and set aside.
7. Raise the oven temperature to 400°F.
8. Spread pistachios and almonds on a baking sheet. Drizzle with olive oil and sprinkle with salt. Use your hands to make sure the nuts are coated.
9. Bake until nuts are golden, about 10 minutes, then immediately remove from baking sheet and set aside to cool.
10. In a food processor, combine the cooled, toasted nuts with some more olive oil, dried apricots, cider and the rest of the honey. Pulse until the mixture resembles a "wet sand" paste.
11. Put the mixture into an icing sleeve or resealable plastic bag with the corner cut off and fill the apples with the fruit and nut paste. Pour on the almond and ginger sauce. Enjoy with an extra sprinkle of chopped pistachios.

ICE CREAM, A PENNY A LUMP

ICE CREAM, A PENNY A LUMP

Ice cream, a penny a lump!

The more you eat, the more you jump.

Eeper, Weeper, Chimney sweeper,

Married a wife and could not keep her.

Married another,

Did not love her,

Up the chimney he did shove her!

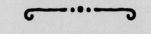

NUTRITION NIBBLE

Holy Cannoli! Kids may scream for ice cream, but they will jump for joy at these Italian-pastry-inspired cannoli cones. Made with sweetened ricotta cheese and bits of fresh and dried fruit, these desserts pack in the sweetness of ice cream without the sugar rush (or melty mess). Plus, fluffy ricotta cheese is one of the healthy, mild-flavored fresh cheeses perfect for even young kids.

MANGO LIME CANNOLI CONES

Makes: 4 cones

Contains: Milk, Wheat

Challenge Level: Piece of Cake

Active Time: 30 minutes

Total Time: 45 minutes

INGREDIENTS

For the Cones:

- 4 sugar cones
- ½ cup white chocolate chips or chunks (plus more for garnish)
- ¼ teaspoon coconut oil

For the Cannoli Filling:

- ¼ cup powdered sugar
- 1¼ cup part-skim ricotta cheese
- 1 tablespoon dried mango, cut into small pieces
- 1 tablespoon fresh mango, cut into small pieces
- 1 teaspoon lime juice
- 1 teaspoon lime zest, plus more for garnish
- 1 pound bag of dried beans

KIDS CAN

- Count sugar cones
- Stir the chocolate sauce
- Dip the cones in the chocolate and set them in the beans
- Squeeze the lime

WATCH OUT FOR

- Hot chocolate can burn eager tasters
- Fragile cones can break

INSTRUCTIONS

1. Fill a medium bowl halfway with dried beans to hold the chocolate-dipped cones upright while the chocolate sets. (You can return the beans to their bag to cook another day.)

2. Combine white chocolate and coconut oil in a microwave-safe bowl. Heat chocolate in 30 second increments in the microwave, stirring in between until you have a smooth chocolate sauce. Dip mouth of each cone into melted chocolate. Set in bean bowl to cool. Repeat until all cones have been dipped. Speed cool-down process by putting cones in the refrigerator.

3. Meanwhile, make cannoli filling. In a medium mixing bowl, combine all ingredients. Beat with an electric mixer until all the ingredients are incorporated and the filling is fluffy.

4. Fill the cones. Put a wide mouth tip on a piping bag (normally used for frosting cakes). Spoon cannoli filling into the bag. Squeeze the bag to fill the cones.

5. Garnish with shaved white chocolate and more lime zest as desired.

MOTHER GOOSE MIX UP

Feel free to swap in other flavors for the cannoli filling. Mint and chocolate chips or cookies and cream are delicious. Lemon and lavender make an elegant combination for more sophisticated palettes. Do what inspires you!

CHAPTER 3

Drinks to Sip

When you make drinks with your "mini-mixologist," give your child time to discover each ingredient. Appreciating "el arte de la mezcla" (the art of the mix) is part of creating drinks that are as beautiful as they are refreshing. After your child enjoys the process of creating their mocktail, they can shake, stir and sip the herb, fruit and vegetable-infused waters. Because sometimes, it's fun to hydrate with something other than water! Cheers!

The following applies to the recipes in this chapter:

KIDS CAN

- Wash produce and pat dry
- Wash herbs and spin dry
- Squeeze lemons and limes
- Twist the zest
- Tear herb leaves (smell the fragrance they leave on your fingertips)
- Crush or muddle fruit
- Freeze fruit to make "fruit ice"

WATCH OUT FOR

- Adding too much sweetener

Inspired by "Curly Locks" on page 151.

STRAWBERRIES IN THE SEA

Makes: 18 ounces (2¼ cups)

Contains: None of the Common Allergens

Diet Type: Gluten Free, Dairy Free

Challenge Level: Piece of Cake

Active Time: 15 minutes

Total Time: 30 minutes

(includes 15 minutes to freeze fruit into ice)

This bright blue beach drink feels like a vacation. Its color comes from the blue sports drink. We generally choose the low sugar or zero sugar option of Gatorade or Powerade to reduce sugar content. Use frozen fruit for ice to boost antioxidant power.

INGREDIENTS

- 16 ounces sports drink (We use Powerade Zero)
- 4 strawberries, sliced in half and frozen
- 8 raspberries, whole and frozen
- 1 orange cut into wedges
- Ice as needed to fill the glass

INSTRUCTIONS

1. Wash produce and pat dry.
2. Cut strawberries in half. Place strawberries and raspberries into the freezer and freeze for 15 minutes.
3. Fill drink glasses half-full with ice.
4. Top with blue sports drink.
5. Remove frozen fruit from the freezer.
6. Add frozen fruit and orange wedges to the glass and enjoy cold!

MOTHER GOOSE MIX UP   Make pretty ice cubes by freezing edible flowers with the water in the ice tray.
See **Flower Ice** recipe on page 223.

Inspired by "The Kettle's on the Fire" on page 137.

CLASSIC AGUA DE PIÑA

Makes: 64 ounces (8 cups)

Contains: None of the Common Allergens

Diet Type: Gluten Free, Dairy Free

Challenge Level: Piece of Cake

Active Time: 30 minutes

Total Time: 1 hour

Literally translated as "pineapple water," this simple, flavored water is a welcome refreshment everywhere it gets hot. I first had it with my friend (and cookbook collaborator) Silvana on a hot summer day in Chile. Slightly sweet and faintly spicy, this drink revives!

INGREDIENTS

- 1 ripe pineapple
- 2 cinnamon sticks
- 4 whole cloves
- 10 cups filtered water

INSTRUCTIONS

1. Peel the pineapple and save the fruit for snacking or make **Piña and Avocado Salsa** (p. 55).
2. In a deep pot, combine pineapple skins with the cinnamon sticks and cloves.
   Cover with 10 cups water and bring to a boil.
3. Continue at a low boil for 30 minutes.
4. Turn off the heat and allow to cool.
5. Strain the liquid and discard the pineapple skins and spices.
6. Taste and add more water if desired.
7. Pour the water in a pitcher or punch bowl and serve with ice.

Inspired by "Kookaburra" on page 111.

VIRGIN WHITE GRAPE SANGRIA

Makes: 32 ounces (4 cups)

Contains: None of the Common Allergens

Diet Type: Gluten Free, Dairy Free

Challenge Level: Piece of Cake

Active Time: 15 minutes

Total Time: 15 minutes

INGREDIENTS

- 1 cup fresh strawberries
- 1 cup fresh raspberries
- 1 cup fresh blueberries
- 1 cup fresh red grapes
- 1 orange, sliced
- 2 cups white grape juice
- 2 cups filtered water
- Cubed ice

INSTRUCTIONS

1. Wash produce and carefully pat dry.
2. In a large (1 liter) pitcher, add half the fruit and cubed ice.
3. Mix white grape juice with water and then pour on top.
4. Top with remaining fruit and more ice as needed. Stir.

MOTHER GOOSE MIX UP

Pour leftover **Virgin White Grape Sangria** into popsicle molds for a frozen treat!

Inspired by "Polly Put the Kettle On" on page 91.

CUCUMBER AND RASPBERRY REFRESHER

Makes: 16 ounces (2 cups)

Contains: None of the Common Allergens

Diet Type: Gluten Free, Dairy Free

Challenge Level: Piece of Cake

Active Time: 20 minutes

Total Time: 35 minutes

(includes 15 minutes to freeze fruit into ice)

INGREDIENTS

- 1 English (also known as hothouse) cucumber
- 2 ounces fresh raspberries
- ½ cup fresh whole red grapes
- 16 ounces filtered water
- Cubed ice

INSTRUCTIONS

1. Wash produce and carefully pat dry.
2. Place the grapes and half the raspberries in the freezer to make fruit ice.
3. Use a vegetable peeler to cut long, flat, wide slices of cucumber.
   Stop when you get to the cucumber seeds.
4. In a short, wide mouth glass, add 2 cucumber slices and fill ⅔ full with filtered water.
   (***Tip***: *For a stronger cucumber flavor, macerate (muddle or crush) the interior portion of the cucumber in the water before proceeding to the next step).*
5. Add fruit ice, regular ice and top with additional water.

ACTIVATED CARBON CAN TEMPORARILY TURN YOUR TEETH BLACK - SPOOKY!

Inspired by "If All The World Were Paper" on page 99.

HALLOWEEN MOCKTAIL

Makes: 24 ounces (3 cups)

Contains: None of the Common Allergens

Diet Type: Gluten Free, Dairy Free

Challenge Level: Piece of Cake

Active Time: 10 minutes

Total Time: 10 minutes

INGREDIENTS

- ¾ cup orange juice
- ½ cup passion fruit juice
- 2 tablespoons honey or agave
- Cubed ice
- 1 teaspoon activated carbon
- 1 cup filtered water

INSTRUCTIONS

1. Layer the juices on the bottom of a drinking glass.
2. Mix in the honey or agave.
3. Add ice.
4. In a separate small pitcher or measuring cup, mix activated carbon with filtered water.
5. Carefully and slowly pour black water on top of the juice.
6. Drink immediately before the colors mix.

NUTRITION NIBBLE

Activated charcoal – also called activated carbon, is a fine, black powder that is odorless, tasteless and nontoxic. While more research needs to be done before we can really sing activated carbon's praises, some swear it relieves gas and can bind environmental toxins such as mold. Bottom line, though we can't definitively say activated charcoal is good for you, in small amounts like in this recipe, it sure can't hurt!

PRO TIP: Cut the peel from a whole fresh lemon (for example) with a small kitchen knife, careful to remove all the pith. To make the twist shape hold each end of the rind between your fingertips, turn each in opposite directions to make a bent, curled shape. Professionals, like my friend and collaborator, Antonio, use a wide mouthed vegetable peeler to get the twist "perfect." Make the twist immediately prior to serving.

Inspired by "Ice Cream a Penny a Lump" on page 187.

GREEN DREAM

Makes: 24 ounces (3 cups)

Contains: None of the Common Allergens

Diet Type: Gluten Free, Dairy Free

Challenge Level: Piece of Cake

Active Time: 15 minutes

Total Time: 15 minutes

INGREDIENTS

- 2 cups fresh mint
- 2 bunches (2 cups) basil
- ¼ cup palm honey (can substitute bee honey)
- Cubed ice
- 16 ounces filtered water, plus more for topping up

INSTRUCTIONS

1. Use a mortar and pestle to make a green paste with mint and basil leaves.
2. Add palm honey to thicken and sweeten the paste.
3. Divide the green paste into 3 portions.
4. Combine the first portion of the paste with water in a blender and blitz to create a murky, slightly foamy green juice.
5. Spoon the remaining paste into 2 glasses.
6. Add ice cubes to each glass then cover with the blended liquid.
7. Top up the glass with more filtered water.
8. Decorate with fresh mint and basil leaves and a twist of lemon.

NUTRITION NIBBLE

Activities that stimulate the senses help the brain to develop and function at its peak. So, help your child discover pineapple with all five senses. Try this food discovery game:

1. Look at the pineapple. Describe how dried pineapple looks different from fresh pineapple. What colors do you see?
2. Now try an aroma analysis. Can your nose identify the fruity and tropical top notes? It may be more difficult to detect the underlying caramel, floral and citrus notes.
3. Combine taste and texture to cover the last two senses, taste and touch. Notice the crunch of the dried pineapple chip, the chewy tanginess of the fresh pineapple and the sweet syrup of the juices.

Food discovery games like this one, are just one way to help your child appreciate new foods!

Inspired by "Robert Roley" on page 47.

PINEAPPLE BASILADE

Makes: 16 ounces (2 cups)

Contains: None of the Common Allergens

Diet Type: Gluten Free, Dairy Free

Challenge Level: Piece of Cake

Active Time: 15 minutes

Total Time: 15 minutes

INGREDIENTS

- ¼ cup canned, cubed pineapple with juice
- 8 basil leaves, divided
- ¼ cup dehydrated pineapple chips (for garnish)
- Cubed ice
- 16 ounces filtered water

INSTRUCTIONS

1. Wash basil and spin dry.
2. Separate 4 basil leaves from stems.
3. Take out 2 tall glasses.
4. Add half of the canned pineapple to each glass plus 1 tablespoon of the pineapple juice.
5. Tear 4 basil leaves and add half of the leaves to each glass.
6. Use the handle of a wooden spoon to mash the fruit and leaves in the juice.
7. Top with ice cubes up to halfway full.
8. Add filtered water to each glass and stir carefully.
9. Decorate with pineapple chips and the remaining whole basil leaves.

𝐂hancaca is an unrefined sugar with a velvety honey and molasses flavor. It is one step away from natural sugar cane and thus retains the minerals found in the plant: magnesium, potassium and iron. This is a specialty ingredient you can typically find at Latin American supermarkets or on Amazon. If chancaca is not available in your area, muscovado sugar is a great substitute.

Inspired by "Curdy, Curdy Custard" on page 179.

MOTE CON HUESILLOS

Makes: 64 ounces (8 cups)

Contains: Wheat

Diet Type: Dairy Free

Challenge Level: So Worth the Effort

Active Time: 1 hour

Total Time: 3 hours

"Huesillos" is Spanish for sun-dried peaches. And nothing is more Chilean than this drink which combines huesillos with "mote" (hulled wheat) and a cold, sweet liquid. The two main ingredients (mote and huesillos) have roots dating all the way back to colonial Chile. Present day, they are the perfect ingredients to make a cool, refreshing dessert drink on a warm South American day. Think of it as southern sweet tea meets a tasty snack!

INGREDIENTS

- 2 to 3 cups huesillos (whole sun-dried peaches)
- 8 cups filtered water
- 2 cinnamon sticks
- 3 tablespoons brown sugar
- 1 package (300 grams or 1½ cups) chancaca
- 2 cups mote (barley)

INSTRUCTIONS

1. Wash the huesillos (sun-dried peaches).
2. Soak huesillos in filtered water for 2 hours (or up to 8 hours) to rehydrate and soften them. **Do not drain the soaking water.**
3. Once the 2 hours have passed, put the huesillos, soaking water, chancaca, brown sugar and cinnamon sticks in a large pot.
4. Cook on medium heat until you have a thick syrup, about 30 minutes.
5. Once cooked, refrigerate until cool.
6. In another pot, cook the mote (barley) according to the package instructions. Then strain and run under cold water to cool. Set aside.
7. To serve, set out several tall glasses.
8. In each glass, put 3 tablespoons of mote, 2 huesillos and cover with the huesillo syrup.
9. Taste. If it's too sweet, dilute with cold filtered water.
10. Enjoy your delicious mote cold.

MOTHER GOOSE MIX UP Substitute ginger beer (this is a non-alcoholic product) for soda water to add even more flavor.

Inspired by "Jack and Jill" on page 221.

VIRGIN MOSCOW MULE

Makes: 2 mules
Contains: None of the Common Allergens
Diet Type: Gluten Free, Dairy Free

Challenge Level: Just a Pinch Involved
Active Time: 30 minutes
Total Time: 45 minutes
(allows 15 minutes for mint simple syrup to cool)

INGREDIENTS

For the Mint Simple Syrup:
- 1 cup filtered water
- 1 cup granulated sugar
- 2 sprigs fresh mint

Note: For plain Simple Syrup, leave out the mint.

For the Mule:
- 1 copper jug per person
- 4 pieces fresh mint (stem and leaves)
- 2 tablespoons hot water
- Juice of 1 lime
- 1 tablespoon mint simple syrup
- Sparkling mineral water, enough to mostly fill the copper jug
- Cubed ice
- 1 tablespoon pomegranate seeds
- More fresh mint and twists of lime for garnish

INSTRUCTIONS

For the Mint Simple Syrup:

This one's easy!
Combine ingredients together in a small saucepan. Bring to a boil and stir until sugar dissolves, about 5 minutes. Once cool, make the virgin Moscow Mule. Store extra Mint Simple Syrup in a bottle in the fridge or freeze to use another day.

For the Mule:
1. Tear mint sprigs.
2. Fill a copper jug with lime juice, ice, simple syrup and torn mint.
   (***Tip:*** *Copper is an excellent conductor of hot and cold, and serving this beverage in a copper jug makes it seem even colder. Make sure you choose copper mugs that are not copper on the inside as copper can leach, yikes!*)
3. Top with ice.
4. Crown with sparkling water.
5. Garnish with pomegranate seeds, fresh mint and twist of lime.

CHAPTER 4

Crafty Additions

These "recipes" allow kids who may not be ready (or willing) to cook to still participate in the fun. Setting the table and sifting flours into a gluten-free blend are important jobs that even the littlest of littles can master.

Your child will be proud to sip drinks chilled by flower ice cubes, hang party flags they made to celebrate an occasion or holiday, and to create original artwork with paint that they mixed themselves.

AXEL, REX AND ME DECORATING OUR HOUSE IN CHILE.

HEY DIDDLE DIDDLE

HEY DIDDLE DIDDLE

Hey Diddle Diddle,

The cat and the fiddle,

The cow jumped over the moon.

The little dog laughed,

To see such sport,

And the dish ran away with the spoon.

Little responsibilities can have big results. Setting the table reminds your child that meal time is coming. Use this activity as a way to help them transition from playing, so they can wash their hands and get ready to eat something yummy.

CUPS OR GLASSES GO IN THE TOP RIGHT-HAND CORNER ABOVE THE KNIFE TIP.

LAY A PLATE IN FRONT OF EACH CHAIR AT THE TABLE

PLACE THE FORK, POINTY SIDE UP, ON TOP OF THE NAPKIN.

SET THE SPOON, SCOOP SIDE UP, OUTSIDE OF THE KNIFE.

FOLD NAPKINS IN HALF, THEN SET FOLDED NAPKIN ON THE LEFT SIDE OF THE PLATE.

THE PLATE IS THE CENTER OF EACH SETTING.

PLACE THE TABLE KNIFE (CUTTING SIDE FACING IN) ON THE RIGHT SIDE OF THE PLATE.

SET THE TABLE

Makes: 1 place setting

Challenge Level: Just a Pinch Involved

Active Time: 15 minutes

Total Time: 15 minutes

Setting the table is a great way to get buy-in on meals and to include your littles in the process without asking them to cook. Not every child wants to cook and, let's face it, there isn't always time. In our house, we keep the kids' plates and all the (safe) silverware in low drawers. This way Axel and Rex can reach what they need, choose the dishware and set the table while I finish up cooking. Since their dinnerware is kid-friendly, if they drop plates, cups or flatware it isn't a big deal. We just pick it up, wipe it off and try again.

INGREDIENTS

- 1 table with chairs

For each person please collect the following:

- Plate
- Napkin
- Fork
- Spoon
- Glass or cup
- Placemat, optional
- Table Knife (this is a non-serrated, non-sharp knife, sometimes referred to as a butter knife)

KIDS CAN

- Do most of this by themselves if they can access all the "ingredients" and reach the table

WATCH OUT FOR

- Kids wanting some help. It's still fun if you do this together!

INSTRUCTIONS

1. Count the number of people who will be eating with you. Don't forget to count yourself.
2. Get out one of each of the "ingredients" for every person.
3. Stand facing the table.
4. Place a plate in front of each chair at the table. (**Tip**: *If there are no chairs or if there are benches, ask for advice from Mom or Dad. If you are using placemats, set them down first. The plates go in the center of the placemat.*)
5. The plate is the center of each setting.
6. Fold napkins in half, then set folded napkin on the left side of the plate.
7. Place the fork, pointy side up, on top of the napkin so it doesn't blow away and stays folded.
8. On the right side of the plate, set the table knife, cutting side facing in (towards the plate).
9. Place the spoon, scoop side up, next to the table knife. The spoon is on the outside of the table knife.
10. Place a glass or cup in the top right hand corner in a direct line above the table knife tip.
11. Repeat for each person who will sit at the table.

BLOW WIND, BLOW

BLOW WIND, BLOW

Blow wind, blow! And go mill, go!
That the miller may grind his corn;
That the baker may take it,
And into rolls make it,
And send us some hot in the morn.

NUTRITION NIBBLE What the heck is gluten anyway? Even with the gluten-free movement gaining popularity, many people are unsure. Gluten is the general name for the proteins found in wheat, barley and rye. Many store-bought, gluten-free flours are a blend of flours that don't have much nutritional value. **Blow Wind Blow Gluten-Free Flour Blend** boosts the nutritional content of the food you're making with it. It adds protein, vitamins, minerals and fiber to any recipe. Switch to making your own and use it as a 1:1 replacement for all-purpose flour.

BLOW WIND BLOW GLUTEN-FREE FLOUR BLEND

Makes: 3½ cups

Contains: Tree Nuts

Diet Type: Gluten Free, Dairy Free

Challenge Level: Piece of Cake

Active Time: 10 minutes

Total Time: 10 minutes

Living a gluten-free or gluten-light life is a reality for many families. While everyone in my family is fortunate enough to be gluten tolerant and free from Celiac Disease (an auto-immune disease treated only by avoiding gluten), we are aware of the challenges many of our friends face. Having a gluten-free flour blend at your fingertips comes in handy. I don't recommend using this flour for breads, but this blend will work perfectly with **Crumble Bars** (p. 67) or **Twice-Baked Birthday Biscotti** (p. 159). I promise your gluten-free effort will be appreciated.

INGREDIENTS

(**Tip**: Make sure all the alternative flour ingredients have the Gluten-Free Certification.)

- 1½ cups brown rice flour
- ¼ cup tapioca flour
- ½ cup coconut flour
- ¼ cup oat flour
- ½ cup almond flour
- 1 to 1½ teaspoons xanthan gum
  (**Tip**: This helps keep our baked goods from falling apart on us!)

KIDS CAN

- Touch the different flours and compare their textures
- Sift the different flours to remove lumps
- Wipe down the counter with a damp cloth after you're done

WATCH OUT FOR

- Sneezes, big sighs, giggles—spilling some flour is inevitable but not dangerous

INSTRUCTIONS

1. Measure each flour.
2. Sift flours together into a large bowl.
3. Use immediately or store in an airtight container in the pantry.

JACK AND JILL

JACK AND JILL

Jack and Jill went up the hill,
To fetch a pail of water;
Jack fell down and broke his crown,
And Jill came tumbling after.

Jack got up and home did trot,
As fast as he could caper;
To old Dame Dob, who patched his nob,
With vinegar and brown paper.

NUTRITION NIBBLE

Which flowers are edible? Well, here are just a few colorful and edible flowers you can add to your recipes: Borage blossoms, Calendula, Violets Zucchini blossoms, Hibiscus, Lavender, Nasturtiums, Pansies, Roses and Sage flowers.

FLOWER ICE

Makes: 1 tray of ice cubes

Contains: None of the Common Allergens

Diet Type: Gluten Free, Dairy Free

Challenge Level: Piece of Cake

Active Time: 10 minutes

Total Time: 1 hour (depending on freeze time)

Like Jack and Jill, your little needs to fetch a pail of water to make this recipe.

INGREDIENTS

- 1 packet edible flowers
  (**Tip**: Just because you can eat these flowers doesn't mean you have to. We usually discard the flowers once the ice melts.)
- Filtered water

  Note: For this recipe you need an ice cube tray. We like silicone trays best.

KIDS CAN

- Do this whole process!

WATCH OUT FOR

- Tiny water spills
- Impatience while water freezes into ice

INSTRUCTIONS

1. Fill an ice cube mold to the half-way point with purified water.
2. Place 1 or 2 edible flowers or flower petals in each mold.
3. Freeze for 15 minutes or until ice starts to take hold of the flower (flowers float) to keep it in place.
4. Fill the remaining space in the ice cube molds with more filtered water. Return to freezer.
5. Once frozen, you can pull out these ice cubes on a hot day and add to your favorite cold drinks.

MOTHER GOOSE MIX UP Add edible flowers to your popsicles, too! Follow the steps but replace water with 100% juice, or a mix of juice and water for a tasty and pretty treat. For a flavorful twist, instead of flowers, place a few fresh herb leaves in each ice cube mold.

HUMPTY DUMPTY

HUMPTY DUMPTY

Humpty Dumpty sat on a wall,
Humpty Dumpty had a great fall;
All the King's horses and all the King's men
Couldn't put Humpty together again.

Eggs aren't just for cooking. The following "recipes" use eggs
in crafts and activities that even the littlest little can do.
Go ahead and break an egg!

Eggs

JUST LIKE PEOPLE, EGGS CAN COME IN
ALL KINDS OF SIZES AND COLORS. THE BEST
PART ABOUT THE EGG IS IT'S DIVERSITY.
THE COLOR, SIZE, FLAVOR AND USES VARY
DEPENDING ON WHERE YOU LIVE.

FROM LEFT TO RIGHT: MY NIECE HAZEL, MY SISTER LARKIN, MARY THE HEN, AND ME. FOUNDERS OF FAT BOTTOM GIRLS MINI FARM

EGG SPLATTER PAINT

Makes: 3 canvases
Contains: Eggs

Challenge Level: Just a Pinch Involved
Active Time: 1 hour
Total Time: 2 hours

INGREDIENTS

- 9 eggs (3 eggs per person)
- Bowl or Tupperware
- Toothpick
- 3 colors of tempera paint
- Tape
- Paper towels
- Canvas (for each person)

KIDS CAN

- Fill eggs with paint
- Tape the eggs shut
- Toss, throw, chuck or otherwise launch paint-filled eggs onto their canvas

WATCH OUT FOR

- Breaking eggs too soon
- Wash hands after handling raw egg

INSTRUCTIONS

1. With the tip of a sharp knife, carefully make a hole in the top of each egg. Enlarge the hole until the tip of your pinky finger could fit inside.

2. Hold egg over a bowl and poke a toothpick into the hole to break the yolk.

3. Turn the egg upside down and shake the eggshell until all the liquid egg (yolk and white) slides out. Repeat until all eggs are hollow.

4. Store raw eggs in the refrigerator so you can cook them later (as desired).

5. Rinse eggshells under running water and set aside to dry (1 hour or overnight).

6. Fill empty eggshells with tempera paint. Use store-bought or make your own, see my **Tempera Paint** recipe on next page. (***Tip:*** *If you make your own tempera, you can use a baster or injector to transfer paint from the ice cube tray to the eggshell.*)

7. Place a small piece of paper towel over the hole. Tape in place.

8. Set canvases on ground (***Tip:*** *Do this outside on the grass*) at a good throw's length away from your child. Distances will vary based on your child's age and ability.

9. Throw, toss or otherwise launch the paint-filled eggs onto the canvas. Watch the eggs splatter and create a one-of-a-kind piece of art.

10. Repeat until all eggs have been tossed. Clear away shells, wash hands and place canvases in a safe place to dry.

Tempera Paint

Makes: 1 ice cube tray of paints

Contains: Egg

Challenge Level: Just a Pinch Involved

Active Time: 1 hour

Total Time: 24 hours (includes overnight drying time)

Long before we put crayons to paper, or finger-paint to canvas, artists used a form of paint called Tempera, where pigment (color) and a mixture of water and egg yolk was used. It's really easy and fun to mix your own colors and paint as much as you'd like. Try this recipe today!

INGREDIENTS

- 6 egg yolks (per child)
- 2 plastic ice cube trays
- Up to 6 colors of food gel coloring or liquid food coloring
- Paper or canvases for each child
- Paintbrushes
- Apron
- Water
- Glass or cup of water to clean brushes

KIDS CAN

- Crack eggs
- Add droplets of food coloring
- Stir and mix colors
- Paint

WATCH OUT FOR

- Food coloring can stain clothes
- Wash hands after handling raw egg

INSTRUCTIONS

1. Crack eggs into a bowl and separate the yolk.
   Reserve egg whites to make **Chocolate Chip Meringue Cookies** (p. 167) or **Pisco Sours** (p. 259).
2. Place some yolk in alternating ice cube slots. Make sure to leave a space so you can mix colors.
3. Squeeze 1 drop of gel food coloring into each slot. Use as many colors as you like.
   Thin paint with water as needed.
4. Stir the food coloring into the yolk to make tempera paint.
5. Use a clean paintbrush to create your masterpiece.

FI! FIE! FOE! FUM!

FI! FIE! FOE! FUM!

Fi! Fie! Foe! Fum!
I smell the blood of an Englishman.
Be he 'live or be he dead,
I'll grind his bones to make my bread.

FRUIT AND VEGETABLE STAMP ART

Makes:	As many pages as you like	**Challenge Level:**	Piece of Cake
Contains:	None of the Common Allergens	**Active Time:**	1 hour
Diet Type:	Gluten Free, Dairy Free	**Total Time:**	24 hours (includes overnight drying time)

Your littles can explore the different shapes and textures of fruits and vegetables making stamp art.

Don't be surprised if they decide to take a bite out of their "paintbrush" half-way through.

INGREDIENTS

- 1 roll paper towels
- Stack of card-stock or white construction paper
- Red, yellow and blue tempera paint
- Fruit and vegetables cut in half to show off their different shapes (We like celery, apple, onion, shallot, bell pepper, citrus fruits, zucchini, starfruit and radish.)
- Apron or paint shirt to protect clothes

KIDS CAN

- Wash produce and pat dry
- Mix paint colors: Blue + Red = Purple
  Red + Yellow = Orange
  Blue + Yellow = Green
- Dip produce into paint and stamp on their paper

WATCH OUT FOR

- Paint on hands and clothes
- Kids tasting the fruit and vegetables.
  (Have extra on hand so they don't eat paint)

INSTRUCTIONS

1. Wash produce and pat dry. Put on apron.
2. Tear off a paper towel for each child.
3. Set card-stock or white construction paper on top of a placemat on your table.
4. Squirt paint out and mix colors. (**Tip:** *We use a bento box and put a different color in each compartment.*)
5. Cut fruit and vegetables so the interesting natural pattern shows (For example: The rings of an onion, the wedges of an orange, the crescent moon of a celery). Scrape out any seeds (like from bell pepper and apples).
6. Dip fruit or vegetable in paint then stamp on paper. If there is too much paint on the fruit or vegetable, dab it on the paper towel before stamping on the paper.
7. Repeat with as many colors and veggie shapes as desired.
8. Lay paper in a non-drafty area or in front of a sunny window until dry (overnight is ideal).
9. Fold dry papers into greeting cards or use as personalized stationery.

WHEN THE WIND

When the Wind

When the wind is in the east,
'Tis good for neither man nor beast;
When the wind is in the north,
The skillful fisher goes not forth;
When the wind is in the south,
It blows the bait in the fishes' mouth;
When the wind is in the west,
Then 'tis at the very best.

PAINTED PAPER FLAGS

Makes: 1 bunting or 8 painted flags

Challenge Level: Just a Pinch Involved

Active Time: 1 hour

Total Time: 24 hours (includes overnight drying time)

Art exploration is fun, entertaining and also educational. Creating painted paper flags supports your budding artist(s) and allows for free expression, an essential component of every child's health and well-being.

INGREDIENTS

- 1 roll paper towels
- Kid-safe scissors
- 4 or more colors of food coloring
- Spray bottle
- Water
- Long piece of string or yarn, about 6 feet for 8 flags
- Glue
- Tape

KIDS CAN

- Tear off paper towels
- Spray water bottle
- Drip food coloring

WATCH OUT FOR

- Food coloring stains on hands and clothes
- Tearing paper towels (they are delicate), but you can always try again
- Rain washing away colors from flags

INSTRUCTIONS

1. Tear off 8 paper towels, or more as desired.
2. With scissors, cut a toothy edge on one of the short sides of each paper towel (optional).
3. Fill a spray bottle with water.
4. Squirt one paper towel with water so it is wet but not sopping.
5. Squeeze drops of food coloring on the paper towel, watch the color spread.
   Repeat with as many colors as you like until towel is saturated with color.
6. Repeat steps 4 and 5 until you have "painted" all the paper towels.
7. Lay paper towels in a non-drafty area or in front of a sunny window until dry (overnight is ideal).
8. Lay your flags side by side with about a hand-sized gap between each one.
9. Set your string on top of the flags, about 1 finger width down from the top edge.
10. Run a thin line of glue on the flag below the string.
    Fold the edge of the painted flags over the string and gently press to glue down the edge.
11. Once glue is dry, tape painted flag bunting in a doorway, hallway or front gate to alert friends that the party is "here!".

CHAPTER 5

Mother Goose Cuts Loose

After dedicating so much time and energy to the health, happiness and well-being of our families, we parents deserve a few moments to relax, reflect and appreciate what an awesome job we are doing.

Mother Goose Cuts Loose is a chapter dedicated to the parents. I've included a few clutch salad recipes to toss together when you're making food just for you, but most of this chapter is dedicated to adult beverages. If you are wondering what wine to enjoy while you eat **Chicken Salad Sandwiches** or are looking for a refreshing pre-dinner drink to celebrate the *happiest hour*, look no further. These drinks will bring out the flavors and enhance the enjoyment of the meals you and your family have prepared together.

Cheers, to your health!

"JACK BE NIMBLE"

Jack be Nimble
Jack be Quick
Jack Jump Over
The Candlestick.

JACK BE NIMBLE

Makes: 1 pint glass

Contains: Alcohol

Diet Type: Adult

Challenge Level: Just a Pinch Involved

Active Time: 15 minutes

Total Time: 15 minutes

A San Diego native, I met James when I first visited Chile - the very same trip where I met my husband Todd. The California Cantina is James' bar and restaurant in Santiago, and I still remember the moment I first tasted this drink. What makes it so tantalizing is the play between spicy and sweet. You'll want to use the spiciest red pepper you can tolerate. Once the Jack be Nimble hits your lips you'll see what I mean.

Note: Serve in a pint glass.

INGREDIENTS

- 1½ ounces Jack Daniels
- 1½ ounces Skyy Passion Fruit Vodka
- 2 to 3 lime wedges
- Dash of simple syrup (see mint recipe on page 209, just make sure to leave out the mint)
- Passion fruit (fresh fruit, frozen pulp or 100% juice will work)
- 2 red spicy peppers (one for drink and the other for garnish)
- Crushed ice
- Sparkling water

ADULTS CAN

- Impress friends with jumping candle sticks

WATCH OUT FOR

- Oil from the peppers getting on your fingers

INSTRUCTIONS

1. Combine all the ingredients except the spicy red pepper in a tall pint glass.
2. This is a mojito style drink. Muddle the ingredients together for maximum effect.
3. Slice the red pepper. If you like it SPICY, add pepper and seeds to the drink and muddle. If you prefer a milder heat, seed the spicy red pepper. Discard the seeds. Add in the slices (no muddling) and stir.
4. Once everything is muddled together and the red pepper is incorporated to your liking, crown the glass with crushed ice and sparkling water.

MOTHER GOOSE MIX UP Swap the sparkling water for ginger beer or ginger ale (both are non-alcoholic). If using ginger ale, use less simple syrup.

PRETTY LADY

Makes: 2 beverages	**Challenge Level:** Piece of Cake	
Contains: Alcohol	**Active Time:** 10 minutes	
Diet Type: Adult	**Total Time:** 10 minutes	

My friend Merrill hatched up this pretty drink - it works perfectly for a poolside happy hour or as a refreshing change for your cocktail. While many men might dismiss this as a "girly drink", don't knock it until you've tried it! This delicious cocktail is both sweet and sour and is sure to impress with its beautiful flower ice.
Note: Serve in Burgundy-style wine glasses.

INGREDIENTS

- **Flower Ice** (see page 223)
- 4 ounces tequila
- 4 to 6 ounces Sprite Zero
- 4 ounces margarita mix of your choice
- Splash of grenadine
- Garnish with a maraschino cherry and/or a wedge of lime

ADULTS CAN

- Listen and dance to *Pretty Woman* by Roy Orbison

WATCH OUT FOR

- More than one **Pretty Lady** in one night

INSTRUCTIONS

1. Freeze edible flowers, like pink roses, in your ice tray. See recipe on page 223.
2. Fill two burgundy-style red wine glasses with flower ice.
3. In a cocktail shaker, add tequila! And margarita mix.
4. Splash in a tiny bit of grenadine. Be careful, a little grenadine goes a long way.
5. Shake together.
6. Pour into the wine glasses. Crown with Sprite Zero (really, there is no substitute.)
7. Have a sip. Adjust to taste.
8. Garnish with a maraschino cherry or lime wedge.

MOTHER GOOSE MIX UP
If your kids are nagging you for a taste, omit the tequila and skip the margarita mix. Voila, you have made them a classic Shirley Temple.

TO MAKE VANILLA SUGAR YOU NEED 2 CUPS SUGAR AND 2 VANILLA BEANS. SEED THE BEANS (RESERVE THE PODS) AND COMBINE SEEDS AND SUGAR IN A FOOD PROCESSOR. ADD TO A JAR WITH THE RESERVED PODS. ALLOW VANILLA TO INFUSE THE SUGAR. BEST AFTER 2 WEEKS.

MUÑOZ MANGO MARGARITA

Makes: 1 margarita

Contains: Alcohol

Diet Type: Adult

Challenge Level: Piece of Cake

Active Time: 10 minutes

Total Time: 10 minutes

Remember Antonio? He collaborated on all the non-alcoholic mocktails for kids to enjoy. What you may not know is he is the go-to mixologist in Chile. Restaurants hire him to develop their cocktail menus. I wasn't ready to let his world famous talents slip away without at least one signature cocktail. Here is his margarita recipe - remastered! **Note:** Serve in margarita glass or rocks glass.

INGREDIENTS

- 3 ounces tequila
- 1 ounce fresh mango juice
- Drops of Frank's Hot Sauce or hot sauce of your choice
- 1 tablespoon plus 1 teaspoon lemon juice
- ½ ounce (1 tablespoon) simple syrup, more to taste
- Ice
- Vanilla sugar to rim the glass
- Wedges of lime or lemon as garnish

ADULTS CAN

- Take a trip to Margaritaville
- Be inspired and prepared for Taco Tuesday any day of the week.

WATCH OUT FOR

- 1 margarita... 2 margaritas 3 margaritas... floor. Don't let it be you!

INSTRUCTIONS

1. Rim the margarita glass with vanilla sugar.
2. Put ice and the rest of the ingredients in a blender or shaker.
3. Serve frozen or on the rocks garnished with a wedge of lime.

MOTHER GOOSE COOKING TIP

To rim your margarita glass, pour some sugar (on me! ♫ haha*) onto a small plate, enough to cover the surface. Fit a wedge of lime or lemon on your glass rim and drag it around the edge. Remove lime wedge, and stamp the glass rim in the sugar.

*For those wondering, this is a Def Leopard reference. For those wondering who the heck Def Leopard is, they're a rockin' hair band from the 80s.

NEW ORLEANS FROZEN MILK PUNCH

Makes: 1 dessert drink

Contains: Alcohol, Milk

Diet Type: Adult

Challenge Level: Piece of Cake

Active Time: 10 minutes

Total Time: 10 minutes

Milk punch always reminds me of carnival season in New Orleans. The season starts January 6th and ends on Mardi Gras day. Our next door neighbors always held fancy-brunch parties to kick off the morning parades. I first had frozen milk punch there. While I don't suggest drinking milk punch in the mornings, this frozen spiked milkshake makes a delicious dessert during carnival season or any other time of year.

Note: Serve in a double old fashioned or cognac glass.

INGREDIENTS

- 1¼ ounces bourbon
- 1 tablespoon dark rum
- 2 ounces full fat milk
- 1 scoop vanilla ice cream
- ¾ teaspoon vanilla extract
- 1 tablespoon maple syrup
- Dash of grated nutmeg

ADULTS CAN

- Bring a little NOLA into their homes
- Enjoy dessert

WATCH OUT FOR

- Milk Punch mustaches
- Brain freezes

INSTRUCTIONS

1. Add ingredients to your blender. Blitz until just combined and a little frothy.
2. Pour into a double old fashioned glass and top with a swirl of nutmeg.

MOTHER GOOSE MIX UP

If you are avoiding milk, or are lactose-intolerant, try a dairy alternative made from almond, coconut or soy. Experiment with different combinations. Personally, I like the flavor of the soy milk replacement best.

Toddberry Mojito

Makes: 2 pint glasses
Contains: Alcohol
Diet Type: Adult

Challenge Level: Just a Pinch Involved
Active Time: 10 minutes
Total Time: 10 minutes

My husband Todd builds blueberry farms, and he is known by our friends and family as Toddberry. When Todd and I decided to get married, my friend Lani wanted to make a signature drink for us. She served it at my bridal shower and we have been drinking it ever since. Are blueberries the key to a happy marriage... we think so. Todd, I love you *berry* much! **Note:** Serve in a pint glass.

INGREDIENTS

- 1 pack (6 ounces) fresh blueberries
- 2 handfuls fresh mint leaves
- ½ ounce (1 tablespoon) simple syrup
- 3 ounces vodka
- 3 ounces club soda
- Ice

INSTRUCTIONS

1. Wash blueberries and mint.
2. Separate the fresh blueberries and mint into 4 piles.
3. Add 1 pile of berries and 1 pile of leaves to each pint glass.
4. Muddle blueberries and mint in the bottom of each glass.
5. Fill a cocktail shaker half full of ice. Add vodka and a splash of simple syrup to the shaker.
   (**Tip:** *this is the perfect place to use leftover mint simple syrup from* **Virgin Moscow Mule** *on p. 209.*)
6. Shake. Shake. Shake.
7. Strain over your pint glass. Add some ice to each glass and at least one part club soda.
8. Stir, then garnish with the remaining fresh blueberries and a sprig of mint.

ADULTS CAN

- Take out any frustrations while mashing blueberry and mint leaves

WATCH OUT FOR

- Mint leaves in teeth from smiling so much

MOTHER GOOSE MIX UP

For parties, make a pitcher of blueberry mojitos and have extra mint, blueberries and ice available for guests to garnish their glass.

LEMON CHAMPAGNE COCKTAIL

Makes: 2 flutes
Contains: Alcohol
Diet Type: Adult

Challenge Level: Piece of Cake
Active Time: 10 minutes
Total Time: 10 minutes

My go-to drink is sparkling wine as I only drink cocktails on special occasions. Espumante, prosecco, cava or champagne—I do indeed like my bubbles. So a champagne cocktail gives me the best of both worlds. It's fun and it's sparkly! Whenever I want to feel less "mom" and more "bomb", I sip on one of these.
Note: Serve in a champagne flute.

INGREDIENTS

- Crushed ice
- 2 ounces London dry gin
- 1 teaspoon simple syrup
- ½ ounce (1 tablespoon) lemon juice
- 5 ounces Brut champagne or sparkling wine
- Lemon twist for garnish

INSTRUCTIONS

1. In a chilled cocktail shaker combine crushed ice, gin, simple syrup and lemon juice.
2. Shake it like you mean it!
3. Rim your champagne flute with lemon juice.
4. Strain shaker into a chilled champagne flute.
5. Crown with champagne.
6. Garnish with a twist of lemon and serve.

ADULTS CAN

- Feel fancy
- Sip with pinkies out

WATCH OUT FOR

- Catching yourself saying, "More champers, darling!"

FLORIDA GIN  TONIC

Makes:	2 rocks glasses	**Challenge Level:**	Piece of Cake
Contains:	Alcohol	**Active Time:**	10 minutes
Diet Type:	Adult	**Total Time:**	10 minutes

The G&T has a distinctive manly man quality to it. The smell of it reminds me of my granddad. I lived with my grandparents when I was in elementary school. When Pop came home from his job at NASA, he'd make himself this cocktail and ask me about my school day. I'd drink lemonade or chocolate milk and tell him all about the important work I was doing in class. Our happy hours always made me feel smart, even though he was the Rocket Scientist. **Note:** Serve in a rocks glass.

INGREDIENTS

- 1 part London dry gin (We like Beefeaters)
- 1 part low sugar Fever Tree Tonic
- 5 drops black currant bitters
- Juice of a fresh ruby red grapefruit, to taste
- Strips of grapefruit peel
- Garnish with a twist of grapefruit and sprig of fresh rosemary

ADULTS CAN

- Make the twist
- Drink this while discussing current events with your littles

WATCH OUT FOR

- Being impressed by how smart your kiddo has become

INSTRUCTIONS

The ratio of gin to tonic varies according to taste. *Pop liked a 1:1 ratio.*

1. With a small kitchen knife or wide mouthed vegetable peeler, cut strips of peel from a whole fresh ruby red grapefruit. Use the knife to scrape and remove all the pith. Set one strip aside for the twist.
2. Fill an old-fashioned glass ⅔ full with ice.
3. Add grapefruit peels and rosemary. Mash with a spoon to release the natural oils and fragrance.
4. Add grapefruit juice, then gin.
5. Crown with tonic.
6. Stir it all together with a spoon or cocktail stirrer.
7. Garnish with grapefruit twist and another sprig of rosemary. (***Tip:*** *To make the twist hold each end of the rind between your fingertips, turn each in opposite directions to make a bent, curled shape.*)

CHRISTMAS PUNCH

Makes: 2 martinis or 2 coupes **Challenge Level:** Piece of Cake
Contains: Alcohol **Active Time:** 10 minutes
Diet Type: Adult **Total Time:** 10 minutes

This recipe is a variation of one shared with me by my friend and mentor Dr. Christie who wrote the foreword to this book. She lives in Florida and serves this festive punch during the holidays. In Chile, as in Florida, we celebrate the New Year under a warm sun. This cool, sweet-tart drink makes the season more merry and bright! **Note:** Serve in a classic martini or coupe glass.

INGREDIENTS

- 4 ounces cranberry juice cocktail
- 1 ounce Southern Comfort
- 1 ounce bourbon whiskey
- Squirt of 1 mandarin orange wedge
- Dash (1 shake) of ground cloves (Not too much!)
- Ice cubes
- Twist of orange and fresh cranberries as a garnish

ADULTS CAN

- Toast the season
- Be merry
- Spread the holiday cheer

WATCH OUT FOR

- Hydrating with water at the same time so you don't feel like you've been run over by a reindeer the next morning.

INSTRUCTIONS

1. Mix the first five ingredients in a cocktail shaker filled with ice.
2. Pour into a martini or coupe glass.
3. Garnish with cranberries and twist of orange.
4. Fa la la la la, la la la la...

PISCO SOUR

Makes: 2 flutes

Contains: Alcohol, Egg

Diet Type: Adult

Challenge Level: Piece of Cake

Active Time: 10 minutes

Total Time: 10 minutes

Both Chile and Peru claim denomination of origin for Pisco, and both countries have their own version of the pisco sour. The Chilean pisco sour (featured here) uses lemon juice. The Peruvians use key limes. All pisco is a type of brandy. It's a high-proof, light-colored spirit made from muscat grapes. We lived in Chile for over 5 years. If you have a chance to travel to Chile, make a trip north to Valle del Elqui. This valley produces some awesome pisco as well as Syrah and Carmenere wines. While you're there, take advantage of being in the world's first international Dark Sky Sanctuary and go star-gazing. **Note:** Serve in champagne flutes (Chilean) or whiskey glasses (Peruvian).

INGREDIENTS

- 3 ounces of Chilean pisco
- 1 ounce (2 tablespoons) lemon juice
  (**Tip:** *Substitute with key limes for Peruvian Style*)
- 1 ounce (2 tablespoons) simple syrup
- 1 egg white from a pasteurized egg
- Drops of Angostura bitters to garnish

ADULTS CAN

- Make Chilean and Peruvian Pisco Sours
- Vote on your favorite

WATCH OUT FOR

- Salmonella. This drink contains raw egg. Check your supermarket for pasteurized eggs

INSTRUCTIONS

1. Place pisco glasses in the refrigerator.
2. Put all the ingredients in a shaker plus a spoonful of egg white.
3. Add 4 to 5 ice cubes and shake vigorously for 10 to 15 seconds.
4. Strain into the chilled glass. Appreciate the luscious foam.
5. Finish with 3 drops of Angostura bitters. Serve immediately.

CHARDONNAY SOUR

Makes: 2 wine glasses
Contains: Alcohol
Diet Type: Adult

Challenge Level: Piece of Cake
Active Time: 10 minutes
Total Time: 10 minutes

If you're not ready to dive into a spirited drink like the Pisco Sour, you can still experience Chilean culture with this lighter aperitivo. The Chardonnay Sour is made with wine instead of pisco, and is a great way to teach people who swear they "hate Chardonnay" that, in fact, it can be dang delicious. I hope you enjoy this drink and find a new love for one of the world's most popular wines. **Note:** Serve in a wine glass.

INGREDIENTS

- 5 ounces Chardonnay
- 3 ounces lemon juice
- 3 ounces simple syrup
- Cubed ice

INSTRUCTIONS

1. This one's easy!
   Combine all the ingredients with ice in a cocktail shaker.
2. Shake vigorously until well-blended and the outside of shaker feels too cold to hold.
3. Serve in a wine glass with a lemon wedge. Add ice if desired.

ADULTS CAN

- Rediscover Chardonnay

WATCH OUT FOR

- This becoming your new favorite cocktail.

MOTHER GOOSE MIX UP

Some people like to put a little spicy V8 tomato juice or Clamato in their Michelada, so it's almost like a beer-based Bloody Mary. If that's your jam, add tomato juice to taste in your pint glass before the beer, and garnish with your favorite Bloody Mary accessories like fresh celery or pickled green beans.

MICHELADA

Makes: 2 pint glasses
Contains: Alcohol
Diet Type: Adult

Challenge Level: Piece of Cake
Active Time: 15 minutes
Total Time: 15 minutes

The Michelada is a beer with benefits. It's cold and refreshing with a little bit of zing. It works best with Mexican beers, and to me there is no substitute for the classic: *Modelo*. Use leftover Creole seasoning whenever you want a taste of New Orleans—or another Michelada. **Note:** Serve in a chilled pint glass.

INGREDIENTS

For the Creole Seasoning:

- 3 tablespoons paprika
- 2 tablespoons onion powder
- 2 tablespoons garlic powder
- 2 tablespoons dried oregano
- 2 tablespoons dried basil
- 1 tablespoons dried thyme

- 1 tablespoon black pepper
- 1 tablespoon white pepper
- 1 tablespoon cayenne pepper
- 1 tablespoon coarse sea salt
- Pinch of chili powder
- Pinch of cumin powder

For each Pint Glass:

- Enough Creole seasoning for each pint glass rim
- 1 lemon
- Dash or 2 of Worcestershire sauce
- Drops of a Louisiana-style hot sauce (We like Frank's Hot Sauce)
- Modelo beer

ADULTS CAN

- Sit outside and daydream about beaches in Mexico

WATCH OUT FOR

- Sunburns. Skin can still burn when you're back-porch sittin'

Note: Zatarain's Creole Seasoning serves as a great substitute for my homemade one. Check your local supermarket for availability.

INSTRUCTIONS

1. Make the Creole seasoning: add all seasonings to a jar with a tightly fitting lid.
   Shake and stir until combined. Then pour some Creole seasoning on a small plate.
2. Scrub the lemon, pat dry and cut in half. Slice one half of the lemon into wedges.
   Set the other half aside for juice.
3. Coat the rim of each pint glass with a lemon wedge then dip the rim into the Creole seasoning.
   Be generous with the lemon juice and seasoning.
4. Add lemon juice, Worcestershire and hot sauce to each glass. Top with beer.
5. Stir and taste. Adjust seasonings as desired.
6. Drink cold.

PIRATE RUM GROG

Makes: 2 rum drinks
Contains: Alcohol
Diet Type: Adult

Challenge Level: Piece of Cake
Active Time: 10 minutes
Total Time: 10 minutes

Jacksonville is just south of Fernandina Beach and Amelia Island, which used to be a haven for pirates, smugglers, and bootleggers of liquor and stolen treasure. It has been said that at one point, there were more pirate galleons in the harbor than local ships. My family loves escaping up there to take in the local flavor, search for potential hidden treasure and enjoy the wonderful beaches. We love the annual Eight Flags Shrimp Festival, and drink where the pirates used to go, The Palace Saloon, which happens to be Florida's oldest bar. Arrrgh you thirsty, matey?
Note: Serve in a rocks glass or your favorite pirate mug.

INGREDIENTS

- Juice of 2 limes
- 2 tablespoons brown sugar
- 3 ounces dark rum (We like Mount Gay Barbados Rum)
- 6 ounces sparkling water, divided
- Crushed ice, enough to fill your glasses

ADULTS CAN

- Talk like a pirate

WATCH OUT FOR

- Talking too much like a pirate

INSTRUCTIONS

*(**Tip:** it do be helpin' to talk like a pirate (yar!) and sling out your best insults.*

1. In your shaker, add brown sugar and a splash of warm water (about 1 ounce).
   Shake vigorously to dissolve the sugar.
2. Add lime juice.
3. Pour in the rum, the rest of the water and crushed ice.
4. Shake. Shake. Shake.
5. Pour over smashed ice. Serve. Cheers, Matey!

FOOD ⟨AND⟩ RECIPE PAIRINGS

If you are wondering which wine to enjoy while you snack on a **Fresh Veggie Plate** or are looking for a refreshing pre-dinner drink to celebrate the happiest hour, look no further. With the help of my local wine shop and my good friend and talented winemaker Amy McCandlish, I've put together a short list of pairings. These drinks will bring out the flavors and enhance the enjoyment of the meals you and your family have prepared together.

Homemade Corn Tortilla Chips (p. 51) **-** Pair with *Michelada*, the bright, spicy lemon better-than-beer cocktail is easy-going and refreshing—like your best friend. Chips and guacamole are my best snack friends... So, what could be more natural!

Piña and Avocado Salsa (p. 55) - Pair with *Muñoz Mango Margarita*—it's the closest you can get to having a margarita in your salsa. And it's perfect for every Taco Tuesday (or Wednesday, or Thursday) for the rest of your life!

Crab Cakes with Remoulade Sauce (p. 57) - Serve with a Pinot Blanc. Try one from the Alsace region of France. Rich, fresh and delicate, these flavors won't out-compete the subtleties of the crab.

Fresh Veggie Plate with Honey Mustard Dipping Sauce and Lemon Hummus (p. 61) - A light, refreshing Pinot Noir will go nicely here. Try it slightly chilled! Look to Burgundy, the home of Dijon and birthplace of Pinot Noir and Chardonnay. Both of these varieties would be great options.

Crumble Bars (p. 67) - Pair with *Jack be Nimble*. Have you heard, "like attracts like"? The passion fruit in the tropical crumble bars compliments the passion fruit in the cocktail. But you've also heard, "opposites attract". That works too, as the sweetness in the bars balances with the spicy drink.

Rosemary Crackers (p. 75) - Break out your favorite cheeses and open a bottle of Cotes du Rhone. My local wine shop turned me on to the Vieux Clocher from Arnoux & Fils. It's full-bodied, fruity, with a big finish and a hint of spice. This red also pairs well with grilled meat and chicken.

Garlic and Herb Marinated Olives (p. 79) - Try to match the salinity of the olives with that of the wine—look to Mediterranean white wines from Sicily or Sardinia. The sea breeze gives the wine just a hint of brininess.

Pebre (p. 83) - Serve with *Pisco Sour* or *Chardonnay Sour* to keep the Chilean theme going!

Southern-Style Pimento Cheese (p. 87) - Try a full bodied rosé from the Bandol region of France or a South African rosé made from Cabernet Sauvignon grapes. Rosés with a bit of backbone and spice will stand up well to the pimento's strong flavors while cleansing the palate.

Chicken Salad Sandwiches (p. 94) - Pair with a Chardonnay. The creaminess of the roasted chicken matches the richness of the oak flavor.

Cucumber and Radish Sandwiches (p. 96) - Earthy wines will match the veggies - you might try a Chenin Blanc from the Loire Valley.

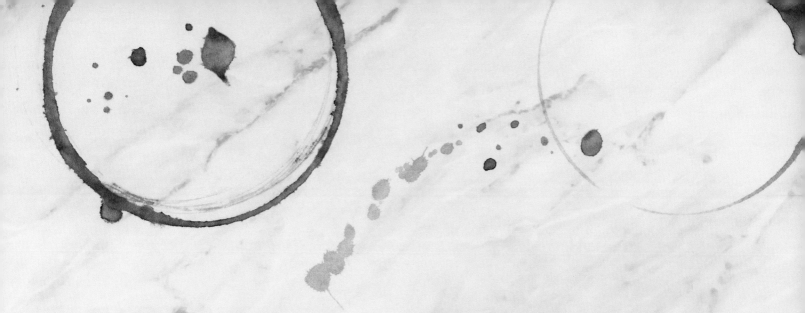

Pimento Cheese Sandwiches (p. 97) - Try some pink bubbles! Sparkling wines like Crémant comes in all shades of pink as well.

Classic and "Crazy" Grilled Cheese (p. 101) - Pair with a Sauvignon Blanc - Try one from New Zealand - the most classic region is Marlborough, but head a bit west to the Nelson region for more subtlety and balance. I like the Sauvignon Blanc from Neudorf Vineyards.

Braided Egg Buns (p. 117) - An unoaked, medium-dry Riesling will go with this sweet, yeasty bread. The Pierre Sparr Alsacian Riesling is my favorite - it also pairs well with *Kale, Caesar!* (p. 275) and *Nectarine Ceviche* (p. 283).

Mama's Apple Pie (p. 129) - While normally I serve coffee with warm apple pie, some occasions call for something a little more festive. Our local wine shop suggested a 2015 Carmes de Rieussec, Sauternes. It's a golden-honey colored dessert wine blend primarily composed of Semillon. It's bright, fruity and beautiful... Just like you!

Chocolate Cake Truffles (p. 139) - Fortified wine, like a ruby port compliment chocolate cake's earthy flavor. Sweet, chocolate indulgences also taste great with big, dark-fruited reds like a Californian Cabernet Sauvignon.

Maple Bacon Cake and Maple Icing (p. 147) - Rich whites like Châteauneuf-du-Pape blanc, German Riesling or Alsatian Pinot Blanc are all great options to cut the smoky richness of the maple and bacon.

Twice-Baked Birthday Biscotti (p. 159) - Vin Santo, made from raisins, is a sweet wine usually served with cantuccini (biscotti) to be dipped in it. The golden wine has been part of the Tuscan culinary tradition since medieval times. It was originally (and in many cases still is) made on farms. I had it for the first time when I spent a summer semester in Tuscany studying the Mediterranean Diet.

Poppy Seed Crepes with Lemon Curd (p. 175) - I like to pair this lemony dish with a Sauvignon Blanc from Chile's Aconcagua Region. During our five years living in Santiago, Chile we visited this wine area located just 60 miles to the north of our house very often. Valle Aconcagua is named after the Aconcagua mountain, the highest peak in all of South America, and while it is famous for producing some of the country's best Cabernet Sauvignon and Syrah, the Sauvignon Blanc from Viña Errazuriz is one of my favorites.

Spiced Apple Cream Pot (p. 185) - Sweet Water Festive Ale. Baked spiced apples are awesome with those limited edition, seasonal beers that come out during the holidays.

GROWN UP SALADS

FRENCH CHEESE SPREAD

FRENCH CHEESE SPREAD

Makes: About ¾ cup

Contains: Dairy

Diet Type: Gluten Free

Challenge Level: Piece of Cake

Active Time: 10 minutes

Total Time: 20 minutes

Elevate your cracker game with this homemade Boursin-like cheese spread. Made from simple, every day ingredients, it spreads easily onto crackers, pairs perfectly with most wines, and compliments any recipe or social gathering.

INGREDIENTS

- 1 packet (8 ounces) cream cheese, softened
- ½ stick (4 tablespoons) unsalted butter, room temperature
- 1 teaspoon lemon juice
- 1½ teaspoons dried thyme
- 1½ teaspoons dried oregano
- 1 teaspoon garlic powder
- ¼ teaspoon dried dill weed
- ¼ teaspoon dried basil
- ¼ teaspoon paprika
- ¼ teaspoon ground black pepper
- Sea salt and more fresh ground black pepper to garnish

INSTRUCTIONS

1. In a medium bowl or in the bowl of a stand-up mixer fitted with the paddle attachment, cream butter and cream cheese.
2. Add lemon juice and spices. Beat until incorporated, stopping to scrape down the sides.
3. Use a rubber spatula and scoop cheese spread into a ramekin or other small bowl. Level off the top.
4. Use your fingers to gently press sea salt and more ground black pepper into the top of the cheese dish.
5. Place in refrigerator for 10 minutes. Serve cold with your favorite crackers.
   (***Tip:*** *Make in advance and freeze, covered, for up to 2 months. If frozen, set cheese out on the counter about 30 minutes before serving.*)

WINE SALT

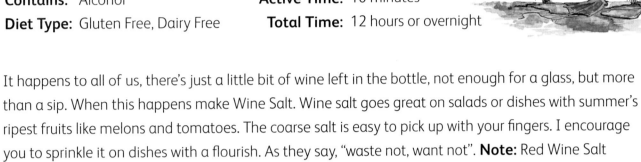

Makes: ¼ cup salt
Contains: Alcohol
Diet Type: Gluten Free, Dairy Free

Challenge Level: Piece of Cake
Active Time: 10 minutes
Total Time: 12 hours or overnight

It happens to all of us, there's just a little bit of wine left in the bottle, not enough for a glass, but more than a sip. When this happens make Wine Salt. Wine salt goes great on salads or dishes with summer's ripest fruits like melons and tomatoes. The coarse salt is easy to pick up with your fingers. I encourage you to sprinkle it on dishes with a flourish. As they say, "waste not, want not". **Note:** Red Wine Salt makes a pretty (and inexpensive) present for neighbors, teachers and office mates.

INGREDIENTS

- 2 teaspoons of red or white wine
- ¼ cup coarse ground salt (We like kosher or sea salt)

INSTRUCTIONS

1. In a small bowl mix the wine and salt together.
2. Spread on a plate or baking tray lined with parchment paper and let dry overnight or up to 24 hours. (**Tip:** *I let wine salt dry out in the oven (do not heat the oven.)*
3. Store in a small jar with a tightly fitting lid in a cool, dry place.

CHOPPED SALAD ⟨WITH⟩ MUSHROOMS

Makes: 6 cups salad
Contains: Milk, Tree Nuts
Diet Type: Gluten Free

Challenge Level: Piece of Cake
Active Time: 15 minutes
Total Time: 15 minutes

INGREDIENTS

For the Vinaigrette:

Use the dressing from Spinach and Artichoke Salad.
Just leave out the artichokes!

- ½ cup extra virgin olive oil
- 2 tablespoons white wine vinegar
- 2 teaspoons Dijon mustard
- 2 teaspoons grated shallot
- ½ teaspoon salt
- ½ teaspoon pepper
- ¼ teaspoon lemon

For the Salad:

- 1 package (6 ounces) button mushrooms, sliced
- Handful (½ cup) slivered almonds
- 2 endive, sliced lengthwise and chopped into bite size pieces
- 1 head Boston lettuce, chopped bite size
- Avocado, sliced or cubed
- Handful (½ cup) crumbled feta cheese, optional but encouraged

INSTRUCTIONS

For the Vinaigrette:

1. This one's easy! Combine all the ingredients in your blender and blitz until combined.

For the Salad:

2. Wash and spin lettuces.
3. Chop lettuces into bite-sized pieces.
4. Slice mushrooms and avocado.
5. Toast almonds in a dry pan.
6. Toss all ingredients together in a large bowl and serve with vinaigrette.

(***Tip:*** *If making in advance, add the avocado and the dressing just before serving.*)

WINE PAIRING

The caramelized onion and prosciutto is a great match for a slightly off-dry, bright white, with similar umami intensity. The back label of many Rieslings contains an International Sweetness Scale - go for medium dry! Try Brooks Wines Ara Riesling from the Willamette Valley in Oregon or the Pierre Sparr Riesling from Alsace. Both pair well with this salad and the Nectarine Ceviche.

KALE, CAESAR!

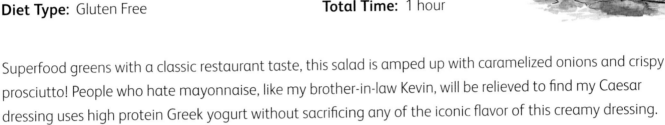

Makes: 5 cups	**Challenge Level:** Just a Pinch Involved
Contains: Milk, Fish	**Active Time:** 45 minutes
Diet Type: Gluten Free	**Total Time:** 1 hour

Superfood greens with a classic restaurant taste, this salad is amped up with caramelized onions and crispy prosciutto! People who hate mayonnaise, like my brother-in-law Kevin, will be relieved to find my Caesar dressing uses high protein Greek yogurt without sacrificing any of the iconic flavor of this creamy dressing.

INGREDIENTS

For the Salad:

- 1 bundle purple curly kale
- 1 head baby romaine
- 1 small red onion
- 1 small yellow onion
- 1 sprig fresh rosemary

- 2 slices of prosciutto, chiffonade
- Crumbled feta, to taste
  (we use about 6 ounces)
- 1 cup Caesar salad dressing
  (recipe below)

For the Caesar Dressing:

- 2 small garlic cloves, minced
- 1 teaspoon anchovy paste
- 2 tablespoons fresh lemon juice
- 1 teaspoon Dijon mustard
- 1 teaspoon Worcestershire sauce
- ½ cup grated Parmesan cheese (The kind that looks like powder)
- ¼ teaspoon salt
- ¼ teaspoon black pepper
- 3 tablespoons extra virgin olive oil
- 2 tablespoons filtered water
- ¾ cup full fat Greek yogurt, natural and unflavored

INSTRUCTIONS ON NEXT PAGE

Note: This makes 2 cups of dressing. Save extra dressing for another salad or make chicken Caesar salad wraps (Chicken breast + Caesar dressing + Romaine wrapped in a flour tortilla).

KALE, CAESAR!

CONTINUED

INSTRUCTIONS

Prepare the Dressing:

1. This one is easy! Add all ingredients to your blender and blitz until smooth and creamy.

Prepare the Greens:

2. Tear bite size pieces of the curly kale from the stem/rib. Be a little brutal as this will tenderize the kale. Discard the rib.
3. Gently twist and tear bite-sized pieces of the baby romaine.
4. Combine leaves in a salad spinner, rinse in cold water and spin dry. Set aside.

Prepare the Savories:

5. In a cast iron skillet, heat a little olive oil - enough to coat the bottom of your pan - over medium heat. While oil warms, dice the onions.
6. Saute onions. Stir occasionally. (*Tip: Caramelized onions are very forgiving. I usually put them on to cook and then get distracted doing something for my kids - the onions never complain.*)
7. Meanwhile, separate the rosemary needles from the stem. Discard stem. Roughly chop the needles. Add to the skillet with the onions. Stir once or twice.
8. Turn your attention to the prosciutto. Carefully peel a slice of prosciutto from the pack. Loosely roll it so it looks like a cigar. Cut into 4 sections. Repeat with a second piece.
9. Add prosciutto to the skillet with the onions and rosemary. Stir and saute together so the flavors marry and the ingredients are crispy but not burnt. About 10 minutes more.
(**Note:** This entire process usually takes me about 20 minutes.)

Assemble the Caesar:

10. In a large serving bowl, toss kale and romaine with Caesar dressing.
11. Add the feta. Transfer contents of the skillet directly into the serving bowl and stir. Allow the heat of the onions and prosciutto to melt some of the feta.
12. Serve with fresh cracked black pepper and a glass of wine.

WINE PAIRING

The oily umami flavors in the salad will pair nicely with a similarly unctuous, medium-full bodied Mediterranean white. My local wine shop carries Grillo and Roero Arneis. Grillo was described to me as a fuller, funkier alternative to Pinot Grigio. The one from Poggio Graffetta is slightly acidic, hits the spot and doesn't break the bank. The Roero Arneis is a little pricier, but a food-pairing darling.

SPINACH SALAD ⟨WITH⟩ ARTICHOKE VINAIGRETTE

Makes: 5 cups

Contains: None of the Common Allergens

Diet Type: Gluten Free, Dairy Free

Challenge Level: Piece of Cake

Active Time: 15 minutes

Total Time: 20 minutes

Every family has certain staple foods they keep in their pantry. I always have jarred artichoke hearts, fancy olives, nuts and crackers in our pantry. This way I can whip out a salad or 'something to pick at' when friends drop by for happy hour and end up staying for an early supper. Adopt this recipe as your "house salad." It's fast, fresh and easy, and feels luxe because of the artichoke hearts. Make the vinaigrette in your blender so the olive oil emulsifies with the other ingredients and has a thick silky texture that coats each leaf like liquid gold.

INGREDIENTS

For the Artichoke Vinaigrette:

- ½ cup extra virgin olive oil
- 1½ marinated artichoke hearts or three-halves (from the jar)
- 2 tablespoons white wine vinegar
- 2 teaspoons Dijon mustard
- 2 teaspoons grated shallot
- ½ teaspoon salt
- ½ teaspoon pepper
- ¼ teaspoon lemon

For the Salad:

- 4 cups baby spinach leaves
- 2 handfuls (1 cup) cherry tomatoes
- ½ purple onion, sliced into "feathers"
- 7 ounces marinated artichoke hearts, drained (**Tip:** *We buy halved hearts in a glass jar.*)

Note: Dressing is even better the next day - just be sure to blitz it in the blender again to remix any ingredients that might have settled overnight.

INSTRUCTIONS

For the Artichoke Vinaigrette:

1. This one's easy! Combine all the ingredients in your blender and blitz until combined.

For the Salad:

2. Wash and spin lettuces.
3. Toss all ingredients together in a large bowl and serve with vinaigrette.

MOTHER GOOSE MIX UP

Leave out the artichokes (everywhere) and toss in slices of crispy-sweet apples, a handful of crumbled feta cheese and almond slivers. Add a spoonful of honey to your dressing to sweeten the deal. Contains milk and tree nuts.

WINE PAIRING Try a Greek Island white wine like Assyrtiko—or even just your favorite Sauvignon Blanc. These wines' citrus flavors, especially lemon, and high acidity pair well with this fresh and bright salad.

CUCUMBER LEMON SALAD

Makes: About 3 cups

Contains: None of the Common Allergens

Diet Type: Gluten Free, Dairy Free

Challenge Level: Piece of Cake

Active Time: 10 minutes

Total Time: 10 minutes

The kids and I love all things lemon and we are lucky enough to have a lemon tree growing in our yard. When I went to develop a simple, bright salad, I went out to the tree and picked some lemons. The dressing for this salad is one of our universal dressings that tastes great on pretty much all summer produce. Try it on a salad of baby tomatoes, fresh basil, onion and mozzarella for a jazzy caprese.

INGREDIENTS

For the Salad:
- 1 English cucumber
- ½ medium onion
- 1 to 2 lemons
- Handful of fresh herbs, chopped fine (We like mint, basil or dill)
- Red pepper flakes, to taste

For the Dressing:
- ¼ cup vegetable oil
- 2 tablespoons white wine vinegar
- 2 tablespoons rice vinegar
- 2 tablespoons granulated sugar
- ½ teaspoon each of salt and pepper, or to taste

INSTRUCTIONS

1. Make the dressing. This one is easy. Combine all the ingredients into a bowl and whisk together until sugar and salt have dissolved. Taste. Adjust seasonings as desired. Set aside.
2. Wash cucumber and scrub lemons. Pat dry.
3. Use a mandoline or a very sharp knife to cut lemon into the thinnest slices possible. Discard any seeds. (**Tip:** You eat the whole sliced lemon, which is why thinner slices are more desirable.)
4. Slice the onion into feathers or thin rings.
5. Cut the cucumber into two-bite wedges or crescent moons. Do not peel the cucumber first.
6. Combine all salad ingredients in a serving bowl. Pour dressing on top.
7. Chop fresh herbs and stir into the salad. Serve cold or room temperature with a glass of sparkling wine.

MOTHER GOOSE MIX UP Use vinegar infused with chili pepper for an extra kick!

WINE PAIRING

The Pierre Sparr Riesling from Alsace is my go to for this salad and the Kale, Caesar! If you're feeling adventurous, try this salad with Moscato d'Asti sparkling white. It's refreshing, very low alcohol (5% to 6%) and will accent the peaches with a hint of floral spice.

NECTARINE CEVICHE

Makes: About 3 cups

Contains: Milk

Diet Type: Gluten Free

Challenge Level: Piece of Cake

Active Time: 15 minutes

Total Time: 15 minutes

In South America, seasons are reversed compared to those in the United States. So it was a hot, hot summer day in February, when we came up with this refreshing fruit salad. I call it a ceviche since the cubes of nectarines sit in a pool of citrus vinaigrette. The juicy, sweet fruit balances the acid in the dressing. When nectarines and peaches are in season there is nothing better.

INGREDIENTS

For the Citrus Vinaigrette:

- ¼ cup extra virgin olive oil
- 2 tablespoons Champagne or champagne vinegar
- 2 teaspoons shallot, finely grated
- Zest and juice (2 tablespoons) of 1 lemon
- Zest and juice (2 tablespoons) of 1 "cutie" or small orange
- Salt and fresh ground pepper to taste
- 1 tablespoon honey

For the Salad:

- 3 firm, ripe nectarines
- Fresh mint leaves
- Handful (½ cup) crumbled feta cheese

INSTRUCTIONS

For the Citrus Vinaigrette:

1. This ones easy! Combine all ingredients in your blender and blitz until emulsified. Taste. Adjust seasonings if necessary and set aside.

For the Salad:

2. Pour the dressing on a rimmed platter. Set aside.
3. Wash nectarines and pat dry.
4. Slice fruit into thin rounds and arrange on a plate.
5. Crumble feta on top.
6. Roll mint leaves and cut chiffonade. Sprinkle on the platter. Drizzle everything with extra honey if nectarines are too tart.
7. Serve cool or room temperature.

MOTHER GOOSE MIX UP Use a vinegar infused with red pepper or shake in some red pepper flakes.

Nutrient Analysis Index

Counting calories is not the focus of this book and I encourage you not to stress over that detail too much. Children need to eat to grow and develop healthily. And, when left to listen to their hunger cues, they're amazing self-regulators, eating more or less as they need. With that said, here is the nutrition information for each recipe as a reference so that you can decide for yourself how to balance your family's eating.

CHAPTER 1: SIT DOWN SNACKS

Kale Chips (serving size: ½ cup or 2 kid-sized handfuls)

Note: *analysis includes pinch of salt but no other optional seasonings*

Calories	Total Fat	Saturated Fat	Protein	Sodium	Carbs	Fiber	Sugars
50 kcals	5g	0.5g	1g	75mg	2g	1g	1g

Homemade Corn Tortilla Chips (serving size: 6 chips)

Calories	Total Fat	Saturated Fat	Protein	Sodium	Carbs	Fiber	Sugars
100 kcals	4g	0g	1g	25mg	13g	1g	0g

Easy Guacamole (serving size: 4 tablespoons)

Calories	Total Fat	Saturated Fat	Protein	Sodium	Carbs	Fiber	Sugars
70 kcals	6g	1g	1g	55mg	5g	3g	0g

Piña and Avocado Salsa (serving size: 4 tablespoons)

Calories	Total Fat	Saturated Fat	Protein	Sodium	Carbs	Fiber	Sugars
90 kcals	5g	0.5g	1g	5mg	12g	3g	7g

Crab Cakes (serving size: 1 crab cake)

Calories	Total Fat	Saturated Fat	Protein	Sodium	Carbs	Fiber	Sugars
240 kcals	14g	4.5g	13g	470mg	16g	1g	1g

Fresh Veggie Plate (serving size: 1 platter)   *Note:* analysis varies depending on ingredients.

Calories	Total Fat	Saturated Fat	Protein	Sodium	Carbs	Fiber	Sugars

No Nutrient Analysis

Honey Mustard Dipping Sauce (serving size: 2 tablespoons)

Calories	Total Fat	Saturated Fat	Protein	Sodium	Carbs	Fiber	Sugars
110 kcals	7g	1g	0g	170mg	13g	0g	11g

Lemon Hummus (serving size: 4 tablespoons)

Calories	Total Fat	Saturated Fat	Protein	Sodium	Carbs	Fiber	Sugars
130 kcals	7g	1g	4g	140mg	14g	4g	2g

Build a Snack Dinner (serving size: 1 cup)   *Note:* analysis varies depending on ingredients.

Calories	Total Fat	Saturated Fat	Protein	Sodium	Carbs	Fiber	Sugars

No Nutrient Analysis

Crumble Bars (serving size: 1 bar)

Calories	Total Fat	Saturated Fat	Protein	Sodium	Carbs	Fiber	Sugars
200 kcals	8g	4g	3g	15mg	32g	3g	15g

Fruit-Filled Ice Cream Cones (serving size: 1 filled cone)

Calories	Total Fat	Saturated Fat	Protein	Sodium	Carbs	Fiber	Sugars
120 kcals	4g	2g	1g	20mg	22g	1g	13g

NUTRIENT ANALYSIS INDEX

Rosemary Crackers (serving size:1 cracker)

Calories	Total Fat	Saturated Fat	Protein	Sodium	Carbs	Fiber	Sugars
60 kcals	5g	0g	2g	55mg	2g	1g	0g

Garlic and Herb Marinated Olives (serving size: 3½ ounces - including oil)

Calories	Total Fat	Saturated Fat	Protein	Sodium	Carbs	Fiber	Sugars
290 kcals	30g	6g	4g	920mg	5g	1g	0g

Pebre (serving size: 3 tablespoons)

Calories	Total Fat	Saturated Fat	Protein	Sodium	Carbs	Fiber	Sugars
35 kcals	2.5g	0g	0g	45mg	3g	1g	2g

Southern-Style Pimento Cheese (serving size: 3 tablespoons)

Calories	Total Fat	Saturated Fat	Protein	Sodium	Carbs	Fiber	Sugars
150 kcals	12g	6g	5g	180mg	2g	0g	1g

Green Sauce (serving size: 2 tablespoons)

Calories	Total Fat	Saturated Fat	Protein	Sodium	Carbs	Fiber	Sugars
70 kcals	7g	1g	0g	105mg	2g	1g	0g

Creamy Chive Dip (serving size: 1½ ounces)

Calories	Total Fat	Saturated Fat	Protein	Sodium	Carbs	Fiber	Sugars
90 kcals	7g	4g	6g	210mg	2g	0g	1g

Chicken Salad Sandwiches (serving size: 1 tea sandwich)

Calories	Total Fat	Saturated Fat	Protein	Sodium	Carbs	Fiber	Sugars
170 kcals	10g	1.5g	13g	250mg	9g	1g	3g

Egg Salad Sandwiches (serving size: 1 tea sandwich)

Calories	Total Fat	Saturated Fat	Protein	Sodium	Carbs	Fiber	Sugars
110 kcals	6g	1g	5g	130mg	8g	1g	1g

Cucumber and Radish Sandwiches (serving size: 1 tea sandwich)

Calories	Total Fat	Saturated Fat	Protein	Sodium	Carbs	Fiber	Sugars
90 kcals	4g	2g	4g	170mg	10g	0g	2g

Pimento Cheese Sandwiches (serving size: 1 tea sandwich)

Calories	Total Fat	Saturated Fat	Protein	Sodium	Carbs	Fiber	Sugars
70 kcals	2.5g	1g	3g	95mg	8g	1g	1g

Classic and "Crazy" Grilled Cheese (serving size: 1 sandwich)

Note: Nutrient analysis is for classic grilled cheese only.

Calories	Total Fat	Saturated Fat	Protein	Sodium	Carbs	Fiber	Sugars
120 kcals	12g	2g	3g	65mg	1g	1g	0g

Blueberry No-Knead Focaccia (serving size: 3-inch square)

Calories	Total Fat	Saturated Fat	Protein	Sodium	Carbs	Fiber	Sugars
150 kcals	5g	1g	4g	290mg	22g	1g	1g

Fruit Leather - Berry (serving size: 1-inch wide roll up)

Calories	Total Fat	Saturated Fat	Protein	Sodium	Carbs	Fiber	Sugars
20 kcals	0g	0g	0g	0mg	5g	1g	3g

Fruit Leather - Tropical (serving size: 1-inch wide roll up)

Calories	Total Fat	Saturated Fat	Protein	Sodium	Carbs	Fiber	Sugars
25 kcals	0g	0g	0g	0mg	7g	1g	4g

Kook-a-Bear Fruit Gummies (serving size: 5 gummies)

Calories	Total Fat	Saturated Fat	Protein	Sodium	Carbs	Fiber	Sugars
10 kcals	0g	0g	0g	15mg	2g	0g	2g

Braided Egg Buns (serving size: 1 bun)

Calories	Total Fat	Saturated Fat	Protein	Sodium	Carbs	Fiber	Sugars
270 kcals	9g	1g	7g	250mg	42g	2g	3g

CHAPTER 2: DULCES AND DESSERTS

Classic Cream Cheese Icing (serving size: 2 tablespoons)

Calories	Total Fat	Saturated Fat	Protein	Sodium	Carbs	Fiber	Sugars
170 kcals	8g	5g	0g	25mg	24g	0g	23g

Mama's Apple Pie (serving size: 1 slice or 1/10th of pie)   *Note: analysis does not include ice cream*

Calories	Total Fat	Saturated Fat	Protein	Sodium	Carbs	Fiber	Sugars
420 kcals	18g	11g	4g	240mg	61g	3g	28g

Chocolate Cake Truffles (serving size: 1 truffle)

Calories	Total Fat	Saturated Fat	Protein	Sodium	Carbs	Fiber	Sugars
200g	9g	3g	2g	90mg	28g	1g	22g

Profiteroles (serving size: 1 profiterole)   *Note: analysis includes 1 tablespoon dulce de leche per profiterole*

Calories	Total Fat	Saturated Fat	Protein	Sodium	Carbs	Fiber	Sugars
90 kcals	4.5g	2.5g	2g	35mg	12g	0g	7g

Abuela's Dulce de Leche (serving size: 2 tablespoons)

Calories	Total Fat	Saturated Fat	Protein	Sodium	Carbs	Fiber	Sugars
130 kcals	3g	2g	3g	40mg	23g	0g	23g

Maple Bacon Cake and Maple Icing (serving size: 1 slice or 1/16th of the cake)

Calories	Total Fat	Saturated Fat	Protein	Sodium	Carbs	Fiber	Sugars
530 kcals	24g	13g	6g	85mg	75g	1g	55g

Strawberries and Cream Ice Cake (serving size: 1 slice of the cake)

Calories	Total Fat	Saturated Fat	Protein	Sodium	Carbs	Fiber	Sugars
360 kcals	23g	14g	3g	60mg	36g	1g	26g

Twice-Baked Birthday Biscotti (serving size: 1 biscotti)

Calories	Total Fat	Saturated Fat	Protein	Sodium	Carbs	Fiber	Sugars
180g	9g	1g	2g	70mg	21g	1g	12g

Best Ever Coconut Cake (serving size: 1 slice)

Calories	Total Fat	Saturated Fat	Protein	Sodium	Carbs	Fiber	Sugars
420g	20g	13g	4g	20mg	57g	1g	45g

Chocolate Chip Meringue Cookies (serving size: 1 cookie)

Calories	Total Fat	Saturated Fat	Protein	Sodium	Carbs	Fiber	Sugars
70g	2g	1g	1g	20mg	13g	0g	12g

Cherry on Top Thumbprint Cookies (serving size: 1 cookie)

Calories	Total Fat	Saturated Fat	Protein	Sodium	Carbs	Fiber	Sugars
100g	6g	3g	2g	15mg	11g	1g	5g

NUTRIENT ANALYSIS INDEX

Poppy Seed Crepes (serving size: 1 crepe)

Calories	Total Fat	Saturated Fat	Protein	Sodium	Carbs	Fiber	Sugars
60 kcals	1.5g	0.5g	2g	25mg	10g	1g	0g

Lemon Curd (serving size: 2 tablespoons)

Calories	Total Fat	Saturated Fat	Protein	Sodium	Carbs	Fiber	Sugars
120 kcals	5g	3g	2g	15mg	18g	0g	17g

Hazelnut Tapioca Custard (serving size: ⅓ cup)

Calories	Total Fat	Saturated Fat	Protein	Sodium	Carbs	Fiber	Sugars
180 kcals	6g	2g	5g	115mg	28g	0g	18g

Spiced Apple Cream Pot (serving size: ½ of a filled apple)

Calories	Total Fat	Saturated Fat	Protein	Sodium	Carbs	Fiber	Sugars
370 kcals	23g	2.5g	4g	100mg	43g	6g	27g

Mango Lime Cannoli Cones (serving size: 1 filled cone)

Calories	Total Fat	Saturated Fat	Protein	Sodium	Carbs	Fiber	Sugars
330 kcals	14g	8g	11g	135mg	41g	0g	31g

CHAPTER 3: DRINKS  SIP

Strawberries in the Sea Drink (serving size: 6 ounces)

Calories	Total Fat	Saturated Fat	Protein	Sodium	Carbs	Fiber	Sugars
50 kcals	0g	0g	0g	65mg	13g	4g	8g

Classic Agua de Piña (serving size: 8 ounces)

Calories	Total Fat	Saturated Fat	Protein	Sodium	Carbs	Fiber	Sugars
60 kcals	0g	0g	0g	15g	15g	2g	11g

Virgin White Grape Sangria (serving size: 8 ounces plus fruit)

Calories	Total Fat	Saturated Fat	Protein	Sodium	Carbs	Fiber	Sugars
180 kcals	0.5g	0g	0g	15mg	44g	6g	36g

Cucumber and Raspberry Refresher (serving size: 8 ounces)

Calories	Total Fat	Saturated Fat	Protein	Sodium	Carbs	Fiber	Sugars
60 kcals	0g	0g	0g	5mg	13g	4g	9g

Halloween Mocktail (serving size: 8 ounces)

Calories	Total Fat	Saturated Fat	Protein	Sodium	Carbs	Fiber	Sugars
90 kcals	0g	0g	0g	10mg	22g	0g	20g

Green Dream (serving size: 8 ounces)

Calories	Total Fat	Saturated Fat	Protein	Sodium	Carbs	Fiber	Sugars
100 kcals	0g	0g	2g	10mg	27g	2g	23g

Pineapple Basilade (serving size: 8 ounces)

Calories	Total Fat	Saturated Fat	Protein	Sodium	Carbs	Fiber	Sugars
45 kcals	1g	0g	0g	15mg	10g	1g	8g

Mote con Huesillos (serving size: 8 ounces)

Calories	Total Fat	Saturated Fat	Protein	Sodium	Carbs	Fiber	Sugars
260 kcals	0g	0g	2g	10mg	63g	4g	51g

NUTRIENT ANALYSIS INDEX

Virgin Moscow Mule (serving size: 2 cups)

Calories	Total Fat	Saturated Fat	Protein	Sodium	Carbs	Fiber	Sugars
35 kcals	0g	0g	0g	30mg	9g	0g	7g

CHAPTER 4: CRAFTY ADDITIONS

Blow Wind Blow Gluten-Free Flour Blend (serving size: 3½ cups)

Calories	Total Fat	Saturated Fat	Protein	Sodium	Carbs	Fiber	Sugars
530 kcals	15g	4g	13g	55mg	89g	13g	3g

CHAPTER 5: MOTHER GOOSE CUTS LOOSE

Jack Be Nimble (serving size: 8 ounces)

Calories	Total Fat	Saturated Fat	Protein	Sodium	Carbs	Fiber	Sugars
230 kcals	0g	0g	3g	15mg	18g	2g	9g

Pretty Lady (serving size: 8 ounces)

Calories	Total Fat	Saturated Fat	Protein	Sodium	Carbs	Fiber	Sugars
170 kcals	0g	0g	0g	10mg	15g	0g	14g

Muñoz Mango Margarita (serving size: 6 ounces)

Calories	Total Fat	Saturated Fat	Protein	Sodium	Carbs	Fiber	Sugars
290 kcals	0g	0g	0g	40mg	24g	0g	20g

New Orleans Frozen Milk Punch (serving size: 8 ounces)

Calories	Total Fat	Saturated Fat	Protein	Sodium	Carbs	Fiber	Sugars
440 kcals	14g	9g	6g	120mg	43g	1g	39g

Toddberry Mojito (serving size: 8 ounces)

Calories	Total Fat	Saturated Fat	Protein	Sodium	Carbs	Fiber	Sugars
170 kcals	0g	0g	1g	10mg	19g	2g	14g

Lemon Champagne Cocktail (serving size: 1 flute / 4 ounces)

Calories	Total Fat	Saturated Fat	Protein	Sodium	Carbs	Fiber	Sugars
90 kcals	0g	0g	0g	0mg	7g	0g	2g

Florida Gin and Tonic (serving size: 6 ounces)   **Note:** analysis of diet tonic water & 2 ounces grapefruit juice.

Calories	Total Fat	Saturated Fat	Protein	Sodium	Carbs	Fiber	Sugars
220 kcals	0g	0g	0g	0mg	21g	0g	16g

Christmas Punch (serving size: 4 ounces)

Calories	Total Fat	Saturated Fat	Protein	Sodium	Carbs	Fiber	Sugars
180 kcals	0g	0g	0g	0mg	29g	0g	24g

Pisco Sour (serving size: 4 ounces)

Calories	Total Fat	Saturated Fat	Protein	Sodium	Carbs	Fiber	Sugars
140 kcals	0g	0g	1g	0mg	11g	0g	9g

Chardonnay Sour (serving size: 4 ounces)

Calories	Total Fat	Saturated Fat	Protein	Sodium	Carbs	Fiber	Sugars
180 kcals	0g	0g	0g	0mg	32g	0g	27g

NUTRIENT ANALYSIS INDEX

Michelada (serving size: 16 ounces)

Calories	Total Fat	Saturated Fat	Protein	Sodium	Carbs	Fiber	Sugars
200 kcals	0g	0g	2g	830mg	16g	0g	0g

Pirate Rum Grog (serving size: 5 ounces)

Calories	Total Fat	Saturated Fat	Protein	Sodium	Carbs	Fiber	Sugars
160 kcals	0g	0g	0g	15mg	17g	0g	14g

French Cheese Spread (serving size: 5 ounces)

Calories	Total Fat	Saturated Fat	Protein	Sodium	Carbs	Fiber	Sugars
160 kcals	0g	0g	0g	15mg	17g	0g	14g

Chopped Salad with Mushroom (serving size: 1 cup, dressed)

Calories	Total Fat	Saturated Fat	Protein	Sodium	Carbs	Fiber	Sugars
220 kcals	20g	4g	5g	360mg	7g	4g	2g

Kale Caesar Salad (serving size: 1 cup, dressed)

Calories	Total Fat	Saturated Fat	Protein	Sodium	Carbs	Fiber	Sugars
260 kcals	21g	9g	14g	800mg	8g	2g	4g

Spinach Salad with Artichoke Vinaigrette (serving size: 1 cup, dressed)

Calories	Total Fat	Saturated Fat	Protein	Sodium	Carbs	Fiber	Sugars
260 kcals	25g	3g	3g	470mg	10g	3g	2g

Cucumber Lemon Salad (serving size: 1 cup, dressed)

Calories	Total Fat	Saturated Fat	Protein	Sodium	Carbs	Fiber	Sugars
210 kcals	18g	1.5g	1g	390mg	13g	1g	11g

Nectarine Ceviche (serving size: ½ cup)

Calories	Total Fat	Saturated Fat	Protein	Sodium	Carbs	Fiber	Sugars
170 kcals	12g	3g	3g	210mg	14g	2g	11g

BONUS RECIPE: Carrot Cake Overnight Oats (serving size: ½ cup)

Calories	Total Fat	Saturated Fat	Protein	Sodium	Carbs	Fiber	Sugars
200 kcals	9g	4g	6g	170mg	24g	4g	13g

NOTES FOR YOUR RECIPES

REX AND AXEL

My two sons love to eat plain lettuce,
so YES—I feel I am the luckiest mom
in the world.

MOTHER GOOSE'S GLOSSARY

Definitions for common cooking terms and the "**Lacey-isms**" you'll find in this book. Refer to this list whenever you see terminology you don't know.

al Dente: Generally used when describing pasta and rice cooking, but technically includes vegetables and beans too. Al dente is translated as 'to the tooth' meaning cooked but left with a bit of firmness.

Bake: To cook in an oven.

Bake blind: The process of baking a pie crust or other pastry without the filling. It is used to keep pie crust from becoming soggy from wet filling.

Bathe: The process by which you bring food (usually yogurt or a whole, raw egg) to room temperature by placing the item in a bowl of warm water as if it were taking a bath.

Beat: To thoroughly combine ingredients and incorporate air with a rapid, circular motion. This may be done with a wooden spoon, wire whisk, electric mixer, stand-up mixer (whisk attachment) or food processor.

Beaten: Ingredients or an ingredient that has been agitated vigorously using a spoon, whisk, electric mixer or fork.

Bind: To add a liquid ingredient to a dry mixture to hold it together.

Blanch: A quick method of cooking food, usually green vegetables, where the item is scalded in boiling hot water for a short period of time and then refreshed in ice cold water. This ensures that the veggie retains its bright color and a good firm texture. Nuts can also be blanched, such as almonds, but I recommend purchasing nuts already blanched versus trying to do it yourself.

Blend: To process food in an electric blender or mixer so that the two (or more) ingredients become smooth and uniform in texture and lose their individual characteristics.

Blow–on–it–hot: The hottest temperature your mouth can stand. Some foods taste better fresh out of the pot or pan. Blow on each bite, test with your tongue and eat as soon as it is cool enough for you.

Boil: To cook a liquid at a temperature of at least 212°F.

Bone: To remove the bone from a piece of meat.
For example, "bone the salmon before serving it to your children".

Broil: Normally a term only used in the United States, broil is known as grilling in other parts of the world. Basically, you preheat the hot rod or grill at the top of your oven until it gets exceptionally hot. Place the food on an oven tray under the preheated grill until it browns and has incredible flavor.

Brown: To cook food until it has an attractive, brown-colored appearance, this is usually achieved by grilling, frying or baking.

Burn: To overcook food so that it is black, crispy, smoky or occasionally, still on fire, and very dry. Basically ruining it. It is almost never possible to save burnt food. It happens—don't sweat it! Toss the burnt mess in the trash and try again.

Caramelize: To slowly cook food until it turns sweet, nutty and brown. To caramelize chopped onion, gently cook it in butter or oil, for a long time at a low temperature, until the sugars in the onion begin to brown and become very sweet.

Char: To blacken something on the outside, purposefully. To char is not to burn. If you've ever eaten a hot dog or hamburger cooked over an open flame, it was charred.

Coat: To cover something with a layer of something else.

Core: To remove the core or center of something. For example, "core the apple".

Cream: To mix fats and sugar together until creamy in appearance. For example, "cream the butter and sugar to make the frosting".

Crumble: A topping (usually for a baked good) with a mixture of flour, oats, butter and brown sugar.

Crush: To break into uneven pieces.

Cut in: A method of blending, usually for a pastry, where a fat is combined with flour. The method often refers to using a pastry cutter (or pinching fingers) to mix butter or lard into the flour until the mixture is the size of peas.

Dissolve: To mix dry ingredient(s) with liquid until in solution.

Divide: To separate into parts or portions. For example, "6 tablespoons extra virgin olive oil, divided" means that part of the ingredient (in this case olive oil) will be used in more than one step over the course of the recipe instructions.

Drain: To remove water from ingredients cooked in liquid or from raw ingredients that have been washed in water by placing them in a sieve or colander.

Dredge: To lightly coat a food in a dry ingredient, such as flour, cornmeal or breadcrumbs.

Drizzle: To pour a liquid over other ingredients usually in a random design or zigzag pattern and often as a finishing, decorative touch.

Dollop: A small amount of soft food that has been formed into a round-ish shape. Yogurt, whipped cream and lemon hummus are all examples of foods that can be dolloped.

Dust: To sprinkle lightly with a powder. For example, "dust the profiteroles with powdered sugar".

Fillet: Most commonly known as a very tender cut of beef, but can also refer to the meat of chicken and fish.

Finger: A measurement that is approximately two inches long. For example, "a finger of ginger".

Flake: To break cooked fish into individual pieces.

Fold: A method of gently mixing ingredients. Usually egg whites or whipped cream are folded into a heavier mixture for a souffle, cake or pie filling. The lighter mixture is placed on top of the heavier mixture, then the two are combined by passing a spatula down through the mixture, across the bottom and up over the top. This process continues until the mixtures are combined. This traps air into bubbles in the product, allowing baked goods to rise.

Fry: To cook in hot fat.

Garnish: To add a small decoration, often edible, to a dish just before serving to enhance its finished appearance. Herbs, sliced fruit or nuts are used as garnishes in this book.

Ghee: The butterfat that is left after the water and milk solids are cooked and strained out of the butter. The only difference between ghee and clarified butter is that ghee is cooked until the milk solids are slightly browned which adds a nutty flavor to the finished product. It's basically pure cooking fat.

Glaze: A glaze is used to give foods a smooth and/or shiny finish. It is a sticky substance coated on top of food. It is usually used in baking or cooking meats where a sauce or marinade will be brushed over the food continuously to form a glaze.

Grease: To apply a layer of fat to a surface to prevent food from sticking. For example, grease a baking sheet with butter or cooking spray.

Grill: To cook by direct radiant heat (see to **Broil**).

Grind: To break something down into much smaller pieces. This can be done by hand with a mortar and pestle or in a food processor. For example, "grind whole spices".

Handful: The amount of food (like herbs, leafy greens, nuts or chocolate chips) that a child or parent can grab with one hand. It is generally expected to be ¼ to ½ cup.

Healthy eating relationships: A relationship which includes relaxed eating, choosing preference over pressure and practicing balance and flexibility in the approach to feeding (parent) and eating (child). This relationship is built from the adult-child feeding relationship and grows with social and emotional development.

Healthy feeding and eating habits: A positive, nurturing environment and healthy patterns of feeding and eating that promote eating habits that are built on variety, balance and moderation.

Hull: Refers to the husk, shell or external covering of a fruit. More specifically, to hull a strawberry is to remove the leafy green part of a strawberry.

Infuse: To allow the flavor of an ingredient to soak into a liquid until the liquid takes on the flavor of that ingredient.

Knead: To work a dough by hand, using a folding-back and pressing-forward motion.

Lick the spoon clean: So delicious you need to get every last bit by any means possible... even if it includes licking the spoon!

Line: To place a layer of plastic wrap, aluminum foil or parchment paper, often lightly greased, in a baking sheet, cake pan or muffin tin to prevent food from sticking to the surface.

Macerate: The soaking and "mashing" of an ingredient, usually fruit, in a liquid or in sugar so that the liquid takes on its flavor. Can also be used to soften dried fruit. Maceration is helpful when making marmalades and the kid-friendly mocktails in the drink section.

Marbling: Marbled meat is meat (especially red meat) that contains various amounts of intramuscular fat, giving it a marbled pattern.

Marinate: To impart the flavor of a marinade into food. This usually requires some time to allow the flavors to develop. Twenty minutes up to two hours are enough for the recipes in this book. This process can also be used to tenderize a cut of meat.

Mash: To break down a cooked ingredient such as avocados into a smooth mixture using a potato masher or fork.

Massage: A quick and effective technique when you're short on marinating time is to put the protein (usually fish, chicken, meat or pork) and marinade in a resealable plastic bag. With your fingers, massage the protein through the bag for about five minutes to help flavors seep in.

Melt: Use a high temperature to turn a solid into a liquid. For example, melt chocolate chips in the microwave.

Mix: To beat or stir food ingredients together until they are combined.

Moisten: To make something slightly wet.

Muddle: To forceably press your fresh ingredients up against the bottom of your glass with a muddler—or wooden spoon to ensure the flavor or juices infuse with your beverage.

Paint: To cover food with an even layer of liquid by applying it with a pastry brush or fingers. For example, "paint (or brush) the pastry with beaten egg or milk to glaze."

Pan fry: To cook food in a shallow layer of preheated oil.

Pat: To lightly tap or slap something with your hands.
For example, "wash the produce and pat dry."

Pectin: A natural fruit-based ingredient used to thicken jams and jellies. Raspberries and blackberries are naturally high in pectin.

Peel: To remove the outer layer of a food.

Pinch: The amount you can grab between your thumb and forefinger. When it comes to salt, recipe analysis considers 0.5 grams to be a pinch.

Pith: The spongy, white, bitter-tasting tissue lining the rind of oranges, lemons, and other citrus fruits. Avoid the pith when zesting or making twists.

Pour: To transfer a liquid from one container to another.

Press: To apply pressure.

Proof: A bread baking term, proofing means to allow the bread dough to rise. The proofing refers to the fermentation action of the yeast.

Prick: To make a single small hole or several small holes, often with a fork before baking.

Purée: To press, mash or blend raw or cooked food, usually fruit and vegetables, to form a paste-like consistency.

Reduce: To boil a liquid in an uncovered pan until it thickens. Reducing concentrates the flavor of the liquid.

Rest: The general term for the time you give food to finish its process. Usually used in reference to meats and doughs.

Rinse: To clean under running water.

Roast: To cook in the oven, usually with the addition of fat or oil. Technically defined as a method of dry cooking a piece of meat (oil contains no water), where the hot air envelops the food to cook it evenly and to allow it to caramelize nicely.

Roll out: To reduce the thickness of pastry or dough by applying equal pressure with a rolling pin.

Sauté: Meaning "to jump" in French, sautéing is cooking food in a minimal amount of oil over rather high heat.

Scant: Meaning "just barely." An amount that's just barely enough. In other words, not packed. When a recipe calls for a scant cup or scant teaspoon of something, don't fill the measuring cup or spoon to the top. Instead, use slightly less than the designated amount.

Scoop: A handheld tool with a small semi-circular bowl at one end to portion out foods such as ice cream, sorbet, mashed potatoes or rice.

Season: To add salt, pepper and/or herbs to a food or dish to enhance its flavor.

Sear (or brown): A method of cooking food over a high heat until caramelization forms on the surface. This is often done before braising or roasting the food, to give it added flavor and is not usually intended to cook the food all the way through.

Separate: To divide an egg into its two distinct components: the egg yolk and the egg white.

Sift: To put dry ingredients such as flour or sugar through a sifter or mesh screen to loosen particles and incorporate air.

Simmer: To keep a liquid just below the boiling point, usually in a pan on the stove. For example, "simmer the sauce until it starts to reduce and thicken".

Skim: To remove a layer of scum or fat from the surface of a food. For example, "skim the foamy layer off the top of the chicken stock".

Soak: To immerse a solid in a liquid.

Sofrito: a Spanish word that means "gently fried." The sofrito is a mixture of 2 to 3 sautéed ingredients—usually onions, garlic, peppers, carrots or tomatoes—that give depth of flavor.

Split: When dairy products such as cream, yogurt or milk curdle or separate into curds and whey. Splitting can occur when cream is added to a sauce and heated close to boiling point. Once the liquid splits it cannot be recovered. Apart from cheesemaking splitting is undesirable.

Spoon Test: Coat the back of a spoon with a sauce and run your finger through it. If your finger leaves a path, the sauce, glaze or curd is ready.

Spread: To apply on a surface in an even layer.

Sprinkle: To scatter a powdered ingredient or tiny droplets of a liquid over a dish.

Steam: To cook food in the steam rising from boiling water.

Stir: To agitate an ingredient or ingredients using a hand held tool such as a spoon or a chopstick.

Straight—from—the—fridge—cold: the temperature of an ingredient, like butter, when it comes out of the refrigerator, about 35°F to 38°F.

Strain: To pass wet ingredients through a sieve to remove lumps or pieces of food. For example, "strain the stock to remove any small pieces of meat or flavorings".

Taste: The amount of an ingredient (usually salt, pepper or lemon juice) you can add to food in the amount that tastes right to you.

Toast: To cook food (usually nuts) in a hot, dry frying pan (no oil or fat) and stir until they are fragrant and golden brown.

Toss: To lightly mix. For example, "toss the salad in the dressing until well coated". To toss can mean to cover food completely in another ingredient. For example, "toss fish in seasoned flour."

Toothpick Test: To see if your baked item is ready to come out of the oven, insert a toothpick into the center or the deepest section. If the toothpick comes out clean or with only a few crumbs, remove the dish from the oven and set it on a cooling rack. If the toothpick comes out with wet dough stuck to it, reset the timer and bake longer. Use the toothpick test when baking cakes, muffins, breads and cookies.

Top and Tail: The action of cutting off the top part and root or pointy side of a food (usually an onion or pepper) to prepare it for another knife cut.

Trim: To remove the edges from something or cut it down to a certain size.

Twist: To cut the peel from a whole fresh lemon (for example) with a small kitchen knife, careful to remove all the pith. To make the twist shape, hold each end of the rind between your fingertips, turn each in opposite directions to make a bent, curled shape.

Well: A method used for incorporating dry ingredients and wet ingredients whereby you make a hole in the center of the dry ingredients, place the wet ingredients in the hole and stir to combine.

Whip: To beat rapidly using a fork or whisk to introduce air into a mixture or single ingredient to increase the volume.

Whisk: To beat or whip a mixture vigorously with a whisk in order to incorporate air into it.

Wrap: To encase one food in another or to encase food in plastic wrap or aluminum foil for safe storage.

Fresh Ingredient Index

It bums me out when fresh ingredients go to waste, so I designed this index to help maximize ingredients that have a shorter shelf life. You won't find the longer-lasting ingredients like butter, extra virgin olive oil, mayonnaise, onion, garlic or canned and dried goods here. These items are less likely to end up in the bin due to spoilage. But fruits, vegetables, some dairy, chicken and seafood are listed in this index for your quick reference.

Most cookbook indexes will list the recipes in ABC order and give the page number where they appear. My index is a little bit different. This index is organized alphabetically by fresh ingredient and then by order of appearance in the book.

WHY?

Because I often open the fridge to see ingredients I need to use up before they rot and then search for a recipe. So when you have a "Whoops!, strawberries are getting mushy" moment you can find a recipe that will come to the rescue (**Tip**: Make **Strawberries and Cream Ice Cake** on page 153).

Use this Fresh Ingredient Index...

〔TO〕 MAXIMIZE INGREDIENTS

If, for example, you make **Piña and Avocado Salsa** and you have some pineapple left over, you can look up pineapple under "P" in the index. You'll find the other recipes that use pineapple as an ingredient (**Classic Agua de Piña, Pineapple Basilade**) so you can make those with any leftover fruit you may have. If your lemon tree is full of fresh, ripe fruit, turn to "L" in the index to see how to put all your lemons to good use.

〔TO〕 STRETCH YOUR FOOD BUDGET

You can also use this index as a meal planner. Look up recipes that have a fresh ingredient you see on sale at the grocery store (Berries! Crab!) to maximize your food budget. For maximum savings, skip convenience products like precut fruit and veg as you pay more for work that's done for you.

〔TO〕 SATISFY A CRAVING

Craving a particular food? If it's a fresh ingredient, look it up in the index to see what you can make to satisfy that craving!

MY TOP TIPS FOR MAXIMIZING YOUR PRODUCE:

 Make stock or soup with veggies that have passed their prime. Find some over ripe fruit? Blitz up a smoothie (or freeze in popsicle molds for a fresh fruit pop).

 Overly ripe bananas add some natural sweetness when added to baked goods or use it to make **Tropical Fruit Leathers** (p. 109).

 Have leftover grilled veggies? Add leftover, grilled, cut up vegetables to the **Fresh Veggie Plate** (p. 61) or add them to a **Classic Grilled Cheese Sandwich** to make your own **"Crazy"** combo.

 Extend the life of your produce by storing vegetables that wilt or shrivel and berries of all types in the high-humidity drawer of your fridge. (If your fridge drawers aren't labeled then both drawers are high-humidity).

 Ugly produce is usually just as tasty as its pretty counterparts. Show ugly fruits and veggies some love and less will end up in the supermarket and farm waste bins. My kids and I make a game of finding the ugliest tomato, avocado, or squash (for example) in the supermarket to put in our carts.

COOKING [WITH] MOTHER GOOSE
FAMILY-FRIENDLY MEALS

Cooking with Mother Goose is filled with delicious, family-friendly recipes inspired by classic nursery rhymes. You'll find a variety of fresh and global ingredients to bring rhymes like *Peter Piper* and *Twinkle, Twinkle Little Star* to your kitchen. Each rhyme is wonderfully illustrated in watercolor to excite a young, culturally diverse audience about these timeless tales. Helpful, expert information about feeding young children is woven throughout the book. Pick up this storybook cookbook and share the fun of making great food with your kids.

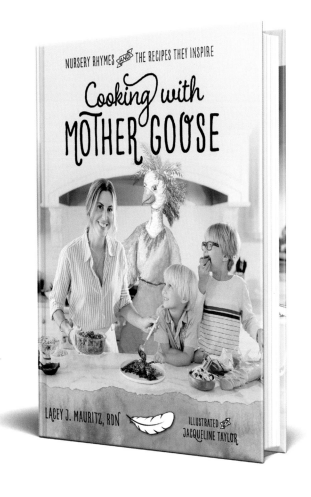

BONUS RECIPE
CARROT CAKE OVERNIGHT OATS

This bedtime nursery rhyme is one of the most beloved by children and parents everywhere. A simple, sweet song deserves a simple, sweet recipe that you can make in your pajamas.

You can find this recipe on the next page, and more delicious recipes can be found in the companion book, **Cooking with Mother Goose.**

Twinkle, Twinkle Little Star

Twinkle, Twinkle little star

Twinkle, twinkle, little star,
How I wonder what you are,
Up above the world so high,
Like a diamond in the sky.

As your bright and tiny spark
Lights the traveler in the dark,
He would not know where to go
If you did not twinkle so.

Twinkle, twinkle, little star,
How I wonder what you are.

NUTRITION NIBBLE In our home, breakfast is the most important meal of the day. Eating a well-balanced meal in the morning helps my children have the energy they need to play, learn and grow. Studies show that eating breakfast has a positive effect on children's cognitive performance, particularly on their memory and attention. And guess what? Grown-ups who eat breakfast get these benefits too! This dish helps busy families like yours get out the door in the morning and put their best foot forward.

CARROT CAKE OVERNIGHT OATS

Makes:	2 jars	**Challenge Level:**	Piece of Cake
Contains:	Milk, Tree Nuts	**Active Time:**	30 minutes
Diet Type:	Gluten Free	**Total Time:**	8 hours (includes overnight refrigeration)

This bedtime nursery rhyme is one of the most beloved by children and parents everywhere. A simple, sweet song deserves a simple, sweet recipe that you can make in your pajamas. I've got a whole other cookbook, *Cooking with Mother Goose*, dedicated to family-friendly meals like this breakfast to help your family eat well every day! In it, you'll find 400 pages of rhymes and recipes like this one!

INGREDIENTS

- ½ cup plain Greek yogurt
- 2 tablespoons cream cheese, softened
- ½ cup rolled oats (**Tip:** *Choose oats marked Gluten Free, like Bob's Red Mill*)
- ⅔ cup almond milk
- 1 tablespoon chia seeds
- 1 tablespoon flax seed, whole or ground

- ½ teaspoon vanilla extract
- Pinch of salt, optional
- 1 teaspoon maple syrup
- 1 tablespoon brown sugar
- 1 large carrot, peeled and finely grated
- 4 dates, pitted and chopped
- ¼ teaspoon cinnamon
- 2 tablespoons whole milk or cream, divided and poured on top just before serving

KIDS CAN

- Measure dry ingredients
- Count the dates
- Wash the carrot
- Stir
- Screw on the jar lid

WATCH OUT FOR

- Sharp blades of the carrot grater can cut knuckles or fingers

INSTRUCTIONS

1. Before you go to bed, mix all ingredients except milk or cream together in 2 medium jars with a tight lid.
2. Refrigerate for 8 hours or overnight.
3. In the morning, open the jars, stir ingredients and top with milk or cream.
4. Enjoy directly from the jar or transfer to a small bowl.

MOTHER GOOSE MIX UP

Customization is the name of the game. You can swap in flavored Greek yogurt. Or add dried or fresh chopped tropical fruits like banana and mango. Like a little crunch? Sprinkle with 2 tablespoons of granola before serving.

LACEY J. MAURITZ, RDN · AUTHOR

Lacey is a food-loving, registered dietitian, wife and mom who is ultra-passionate about child and family nutrition. Her goal is to engage parents and their little ones in the process of preparing, cooking and—the best part—eating fresh, healthy food. This is her fourth cookbook.

Lacey lives in Jacksonville, Florida, and when away from her kitchen, enjoys spending time with her family, playing tennis, and traveling.

For more information, please visit www.storybooknutrition.com

© 2020 Storybook Nutrition, LLC
Printed in Canada
ISBN 978-1-7349520-2-5 (print) / 978-1-7349520-1-8 (digital)

Author: Lacey J. Mauritz, RDN
Illustrators: Jacqueline Taylor and Martin Ortega
Designer: Stockton Eller
Food Photography: Lorena Salinas and Sarah Eddy
Cover Photography: Sarah Eddy
Editor: Sarah Zerkel